COMPETENCE, COURAGE, AND CHANGE
An Approach to Family Therapy

David B. Waters, Ph.D.

Associate Professor of Family Medicine
University of Virginia Health Sciences Center

Edith C. Lawrence, Ph.D.

Associate Professor
Curry Programs in Clinical and School Psychology
University of Virginia

W. W. Norton & Company
New York   London

Printed in the United States of America.

First Edition

The text of this book was composed in 11/13 Sabon. Composition by Bytheway Typesetting Services, Inc. Manufacturing by Haddon Craftsmen.

Library of Congress Cataloging-in-Publication Data

Waters, David B. (David Brooks), 1943–
    Competence, courage, and change : an approach to family therapy /
David B. Waters, Edith C. Lawrence.
        p.   cm.
    "A Norton professional book."
    Includes bibliographical references and index.
    ISBN 0-393-70139-5
    1. Family psychotherapy. 2. Family psychotherapy—Philosophy.
3. Adjustment (Psychology) I. Lawrence, Edith C. II. Title.
    [DNLM: 1. Family Therapy—methods.   WM 430.5.F2 W329c 1993]
RC488.5.W39   1993
616.89'156—dc20   DNLM/DLC   93-718   CIP
for Library of Congress

W.W. Norton & Company, Inc., 500 Fifth Avenue, New York, N.Y. 10110

W.W. Norton & Company, Ltd., 10 Coptic Street, London WC1A 1PU

1 2 3 4 5 6 7 8 9 0

A NORTON PROFESSIONAL BOOK

To Bitsy and Fran
who have taught us the most
about competence and courage

ACKNOWLEDGMENTS

WE HAVE BEEN HELPED by many people in the process of bringing this book to fruition. Many of our students have wrestled with the concepts and their clinical manifestations, helping us to think more clearly and be fully accountable for our ideas. Tom Collins and Connie Caldwell worked on early written forms of the theoretical notions. Cindy Walters and AnneMarie Comber wrote endless notes on our deliberations, and gave useful feedback. Michael Nichols provided enormously helpful reviews, first of an early version and later of the whole manuscript. We are much in his debt. We are also indebted to David Scherer, Ken Webster, Susan McClung, and Bill Gunn for thoughtful and insightful reviews.

The help of our consultation group over the years is vast and inestimable. It is difficult to name all the people who have contributed to our work, but our sense of indebtedness moves us to try. Steve Greenstein has led the way. Sharon Beckman-Brindley, Bob Marvin, Sue Molumphy, Allie Rudolph, and Quinn Sale have all made vital contributions and critiques of various sorts. Ruth Ball, Molly Brunk, Sharon Chilcote-Doner, Margery Daniel, Tom DeMaio, David Dyer, John Freeman, Marney Gibbs, Blackie Gordon, Joe Jackson, Joanne Kittredge, Phyllis Koch-Sheras, Sherry

Kraft, Annie Krochalis, Skip Montgomery, Mike O'Connor, Annelise Petry, Bob Rannigan, John Schroll, Peter Sheras, Craig Villalon, Jane Weldon-Stewart, and Frances Winfrey have worked with us over the years on those ideas, with our cases and theirs. We are probably missing some people, and we apologize. The group has been fluid: some people have joined and some have left since the heart of the work was done.

In addition, we are grateful to three great typists: Barbara Roberts, for keeping drafts moving toward completion, Rosemary Knight, for endless late nights of deciphering yet another rewrite, and Jeanne Stovall, for typing excellence and a keen editorial eye. The most stalwart and long-standing of our supporters has been Susan Barrows Munro, our editor. Her combination of encouragement and belief in our ideas has made us grateful to be under her guidance.

Finally, and most importantly, our deep and lasting gratitude to our spouses and children for their patience, good humor, and love. Without their tolerance and kindness about long absences and frequent distractions, we would have given up long ago. To Bitsy, Claire, Kate, and Eliza Waters and to Fran, Jenna, Meredith, and Avery Lawrence, we thank you for your support of us and "the book."

PREFACE

THIS BOOK IS THE product of many years' work with an extraordinary mentor and a wonderful group of colleagues. Since 1980, we have been meeting monthly with Steve Greenstein, from Philadelphia, and a group of about 25 therapists from all over Virginia. In the group we share cases, seek supervision, and provide support and friendship. Many useful and enriching ideas and relationships have emerged from it; many cases have gone better for it. And always the driving force has been Steve's spirit and vision. He believes that therapy is principally a process of reconnecting people with their healthy underlying strivings: Search for those strivings and you will find them. But the search and reconnecting must be done with realism, hope, courage, and partnership.

Steve's fundamental belief in people's capacity and desire for love and mastery has inspired us to work from the same basis. We have experienced in his supervision what it is like to be seen in this positive light and have watched our clients benefit when that philosophy is applied to them. His brilliance and spirit are the very core of this book, both its energy and its ideas, and we hope we have done him justice.

The group that has formed around him has been almost equally inspirational and supportive to our growth. We have profited from a spirit of openness, direct exchange, and noncompetitive challenge. People have taken tremendous risks in the group, and the rewards have been plentiful. There is a high level of competence and courage that has both challenged and strengthened us all.

For us, the group under Steve's guidance has been an exercise in partnership. We have been helped to try out ideas, clarify our thinking, and expand our horizons. Most of all, our colleagues have encouraged us, in the literal sense, to put the ideas that we struggle with as a body down on paper. That atmosphere of courage, risk, and partnership has enriched us personally for years, and is a prime source of energy for this book. We are painfully aware of the difficulty of reproducing the richness and range of these discussions in print. However successful we have been, we are better therapists for Steve's leadership, the group's collaboration, and for the process of working together as a pair to write down what we have all worked on together as a group. The spirit of competence, courage, and change as we understand them was conceived in and nourished by this group; their partnership has helped us share it with you.

CONTENTS

CONTENTS

INTRODUCTION

THE MENTAL HEALTH FIELD in general and family therapy in particular have increasingly been moving away from an illness-based model of human problems. This book is a part of that movement. Much of family therapy today attempts to address people's struggles with everyday life and its burdens. The emphasis of the field has shifted from analyzing a particular illness and its concomitants to empowering people and developing their coping abilities. Even those working with families with serious pathology (psychoses and the physiologically-mediated mental disorders) place less emphasis on delineating the psychopathology and more on developing and utilizing whatever resources might exist in the system.

For a long time, however, family therapists have been better at mocking the medical model than they have been at replacing it with a new model. Certainly there have been some very substantial new models introduced: structural family therapy, strategic family therapy, and Bowenian family therapy have probably been the best known and most followed. They, along with several other models, have served us all well. But no model has produced a clear, well-defined replacement for the centerpiece of psychopathology and illness: different ways of working with psychopathology, surely — but not different ways of construing it.

As our work evolved, we found ourselves struggling to name and organize our difficulty with the ideas of psychopathology, illness, and dysfunction. Those had been the central issues in the theories we were both brought up on, but they became less and less relevant to anything we did in therapy. The things that others pointed out or focused on as psychopathology usually seemed to us to be dysfunctional patterns *over a base of healthy strivings*. We felt moved to look past the pathology to the distorted healthy impulses underneath, and to develop those. We said to students, "People come by their problems honestly. Find out what they were striving for when they developed the dysfunctional pattern."

Sometimes we have been accused of being Pollyannaish apologists for clients, blind to their illnesses, and hopelessly naive about their prospects. Sometimes we worried that our accusers were right. But we knew we weren't just apologists. We were challenging our clients early and often to do better; we were not just normalizing their inadequacies. We were not ducking the struggle: We were coming at it from a different angle than before. And we were pleased with the results. Our clients were more engaged, more active, and more committed to change than in a psychopathology-based system. But what were we doing? How should we construe our basic operation?

The concept of competence was largely born out of watching children's attempts to master their world. Robert White's work was inspirational in this regard. Children are interested in all kinds of possibilities and in what they can do with those possibilities. So, too, are adults, although sometimes their hopefulness and striving become overwhelmed by life's struggles. We came to construe our task in therapy as discovering our clients' underlying competence and helping them reconnect with their inherent energy for mastery and belonging.

As we made searching for health and competence a higher priority, we became more skilled at finding and enriching that part of people. We were not always successful. Sometimes we were blind to people's underlying health; at other times we overestimated it. Yet it was more rewarding to challenge people to do their best, and sometimes lose, than to succeed at treating them cautiously and apprehensively. Eventually we learned that both aspects of people, their health and their pathology, needed to be recognized and appreciated before they felt joined enough with us to trust our lead.

Competence has become our watchword. It is not a perfect word, and it does not capture the intensity of our best work. But when we construe it to mean an underlying striving, a striving especially for mastery and belonging, we feel it conveys the central focus of our way of working. Where pathology, insight, and interpretation used to be, we place competence and the pursuit of mastery and belonging. Where a retrospective view of what went wrong used to be, we place a proactive focus on what needs to go differently.

The idea of competence enhancement as part of family therapy is not new. It showed up in the work of Minuchin and his cohorts early on and was often central to their work. No one saw it as much more than a sidelight of a larger restructuring process, however. It slowly occurred to us that it was fundamental, and it became the guiding inspiration of our work. We were working time and again to locate and organize therapy around the healthy, striving part of people. Our work has come to be based on what our clients could do or needed to do to grow, and we focused on developing the courage in both client and therapist to pursue that path.

In developing the construct of competence, it is important not to overdevelop it. It is not a comprehensive theory or a new technique for working with people. We take the term "approach" in our subtitle very seriously: The competence orientation is how we *approach* therapy. It is the direction from which we choose to start to understand people and their problems. Competence is our *bias*. We find that this approach brings out the part of our clients and ourselves that we like most to work with, and with which we have the most success—and the most fun. We can ask more of our clients precisely because we have become more aware of their capabilities.

What we try to do in this book is to organize and develop the variety of ways that competence can be used to understand and to enhance therapy. We often tell people in teaching this approach that we will not teach them anything really new. Instead, we will help them to make better use of what they already know.

Early on, that sense of "nothing new" almost stopped us from writing this book. We did persevere, obviously, and as we did, we discovered that "nothing new" was good news, not bad. It reflects the extent to which competence and courage are common, and commonsense, variables. People naturally use a competence approach in raising their children, strengthening their relationships, and dealing with their families of origin. It is a human tendency because it is sensible and humane. In that way, a competence approach to therapy is closer to "real life" than many other approaches.

All of us have gone to workshops and been taught complex systems of therapy that are elegant and elaborate, even if sometimes counterintuitive. However, we have found that when we get away from the training site and work again with our own clients in our own settings that, over time, we revert to our natural proclivities. What worked brilliantly in a demonstration (e.g., paradox, trance, invariant prescription) turned out to be very hard to organize ongoing therapy around. Our tendency, and we think others' as well, has been to include some of the thinking from such training, but to return to a way of working that feels natural and honest to us. In the end, our mode of doing therapy must represent us in a fundamental way. We have come to trust the human striving for mastery and belonging as a guide for ourselves and our clients.

In writing this approach down, we have been aware again and again of our debt to many others who have tilled and are tilling the same ground. We have mentioned some of the giants whose work has inspired us: Erickson, Satir, Minuchin, and solution-oriented theorists, for example. We have struggled with how to include others—the cases or ideas heard at workshops that set us thinking, the conversations with colleagues that challenged our assumptions. Many family therapists' thinking, writing, and speaking have informed ours strongly. We acknowledge with gratitude and humility our debt to their contributions and look forward to the creativity that will take this way of working with people the next step.

Charlottesville, Virginia
September, 1992

one

THE FAMILY AS HERO:
COMPETENCE AND COURAGE
IN FAMILY THERAPY

*Tell me to what you pay attention and I will tell you who
you are.*

— Ortega y Gassett

SONNY, 13, WAS BROUGHT to the clinic by his mother, Brenda, and his stepfather of 10 years, Jesse. They were referred by the Juvenile Court after Sonny was put on probation for vandalism and stealing at several construction sites. Sonny made a shocking contrast with his rural, "country style" parents. He had a half-shaven head and wore heavy metal attire. Though the entire family had been asked to come, Sonny's 16-year-old brother, John, did not appear.

Sonny was surly and challenging from the beginning. The parents were as worried about his general decline—school failures, fights, rebellions at home, and his appearance—as they were about the stealing. Sonny downplayed it all and said there was nothing wrong; therapy was a waste of time. He seemed more interested in his own reflection in the one-way mirror than in anything anyone of us might have to say. The intake counselor challenged his cavalier attitude, given the serious nature of the problems, and Sonny became silent.

Stepfather and mother anxiously filled the silence. Brenda said that Sonny, who had been a terror for about the last year, had always been difficult, even as a baby. Jesse added that Sonny tested them "every minute of every day," apparently referring to his dress and demeanor as much as to his behavior. They both said they had "about given up," and threatened to send him to a youth home if he didn't straighten up. Jesse was more outspoken in his concern and disgust than Brenda. The interview became more and more tense as Sonny increasingly withdrew and the parents presented their litany of complaints. The therapist tried to head off the hostility and get each parent to draw Sonny out, but without success. The therapist's own attempts to get Sonny talking were only marginally more successful; the parents had a "see what we mean?" look on their face as the therapist tried and failed.

The intake therapist's long report described Sonny as hostile, hostile-dependent, a conduct disorder, oppositional, depressed, acting out, incommunicative, resistant, and immature. The parents were variously described as dour, withholding, depressed, resistant, angry, frustrated, tense, unloving, and overwhelmed. A tentative diagnosis of conduct disorder with depressive features was made about Sonny. The parents were assessed as "too depressed and angry to be workable in family therapy," and individual therapy for Sonny was recommended to see if he could work through his lifelong rage at his parents. Adjunctive supportive therapy was recommended for the parents. "Prognosis: Guarded."

Competence

As was the case with Sonny's intake therapist, we do not expect enough of people or of therapy. In general, the errors in all forms of therapy are the same: We do not engage the participants or the issues actively enough. We muddle around and track the client's distress, rather than think creatively about how they might change it. Often we tolerate a level of misery and confusion that we could address in a more direct and helpful way.

The central tenet of a competence approach is to challenge people's dysfunction directly, but in a way that engages their competent impulses as the active element. We can push people very hard if we push them in a direction that has a way out. If we push them in a direction that is a dead end or has no possibility for creative action, then the challenging push is stifling instead of enlivening. But to give people simultaneously a challenge to do better and a map that makes use of their own abilities is, literally, encouraging. It gives people courage to try to use themselves in a different and better way to get out of where they are stuck.

As therapists, we often get preoccupied with the dysfunctional patterns people are embedded in and never look to the proactive question of what they need to accomplish in order to do better. Therapy has an excellent repertoire for the retrospective view of how things went wrong. It has a much weaker prospective repertoire. Therapy has always been good at focusing on what to move *away from*, but weak on what to move *towards*.

In large part, this is because therapists have always been warned against giving advice, directing people's lives, or trying to solve people's problems in any direct way. That is a sensible and appropriate caution. But like many appropriate cautions in the field of psychotherapy, it has been overused. The caution not to give advice or solutions became a much broader interdiction against any kind of direct engagement with the presenting problem or any focus on successful adaptation. Historically, only intrapsychic, unconscious, psychopathological material was thought worthy of the therapist's attention. Encouragment of developmental progress, healthy reactions, or competent life management were killed with the same stroke that eliminated advice and decisions. With few exceptions, no vocabulary or armamentarium was developed to help therapists look at healthy processes, successful adaptation, or personal resources.

Two main issues led to that bias. One was the fundamental emphasis Freud and his disciples placed on the psychopathological process. They believed that man was basically a creature of instinct and primal conflict. While they distinguished between healthy adaptations to this conflict such as successful sublimations and neurotic adaptations, clearly more attention and energy was given to understanding the latter. In fact, there was a strong bias that adaptive, resourceful, successful behavior was a cover to be gotten beneath, not a valid field of study. The *real* measure of man was in the pathological layers beneath the apparent competence on the surface.

The second main issue leading to the bias was that most ways of thinking or talking about resources and strengths seemed superficial and simplistic. Psychopathological events were intriguing and dramatic; they seemed more real. The drama of oedipal struggles or murderous impulses was compelling. The same could not be said of more normal, healthy behaviors. The drive to do well, manage effectively, and develop in a healthy way was no match for the intense *Sturm und Drang* of unconscious forces. As a result, no lexicon of words or maneuvers evolved in therapy to deal with the positive side of human behavior. The striving, hopeful impulses towards mastery and belonging that drive people every bit as strongly as — we would say more than — the psychopathological motives were largely ignored.

So psychotherapy developed with a powerful bias towards the pathological and a dearth of countervailing concepts. We arrived in the modern era with little knowledge of positive, productive, healthy human functioning. Our work is built on a particular way of addressing that deficit and thinking about human resources.

A competence framework views symptoms as *adaptive attempts gone awry*, rather than as expressions of innate illness or inadequacy. It searches for the healthy impulse that resides behind all maladaptive behavior. And it empowers the family to deal directly with the problem in order to recapture the underlying healthy striving that the problem represents.

"Sonny, Part Two"   A competence-oriented therapist was assigned to work with Sonny. In spite of the gloomy report, he was intrigued by the family situation and began to search for the healthy energy in the system. He noticed, for example, that Jesse, a 30-year-old bachelor, had married a young divorcee with two young, rambunctious boys. Was he drawn to the challenge of this? Did he have hopes of rescuing this family? If so, his negative attitude toward Sonny might be about frustrated hopes, not disdain and disgust. Further, the therapist noted that Jesse's plan to help the family had had some success; overall they had done well until the last year. What kind of connection had Jesse made with Sonny over that period? And the therapist was very curious about John, the absent older brother: Who was he allied with? Had he "gone country" with Jesse, or heavy metal with his brother? Was

Sonny isolated in the family (which might suggest the need to reconnect him) or was there solidarity between the brothers? There were lots of possibilities in the family that had been overlooked. Despite the pessimistic prognosis from the intake worker, the therapist requested that all four members come for the first family meeting. They reluctantly complied.

John's appearance answered one of the therapist's questions immediately. In a marvel of pseudoheredity, John looked and carried himself just like his stepfather. He was "country" through and through, and Jesse was clearly proud of him. Sonny, on the other hand, had developed a negative identification process. Finding a positive place for Sonny in the family would be important; as long as he felt isolated he would continue to fight the family by rejecting their values.

Accordingly, the therapist started pursuing the ways that Jesse's entrance into the family affected everyone. Sonny didn't recall anything about it; John recalled welcoming Jesse with open arms and "feeling like he was my real Daddy from the start." Sonny reluctantly reported that he "got along OK" with Jesse but never felt that Jesse really liked him.

Jesse described "trying everything" (e.g., fishing, hunting, fixing bikes) to get Sonny more engaged, but with mostly frustration as a result. Asked if it hurt, Jesse said, "It sure did! I knocked myself out for these two, after how their real daddy done them, and I felt like I was half way failin'!" And Sonny? "I didn't feel like he cared about me. I thought he just wanted Momma, and he was kissin' *her* butt by doing stuff with us." Mother broke in, laughing, "Are you crazy? I always told him he just married me to get to you two! He wanted sons, a whole family, not just me." Sonny's "conduct disorder" slowly began to emerge not as a "repetitive pattern of aggressive conduct" (*DSM-III-R*), but as difficulty knowing how to connect with people, especially Jesse. It stemmed from caution about being used and difficulty feeling lovable, rather than from a lack of empathy for others or a disinterest in relationships.

But this can't be discovered if the right questions aren't asked. In order to discover the health in underlying strivings, one has to assume they are there and ask the right questions to bring them to light. If one searches for pathology, one finds it. If one searches for competence, one finds that as well. And the two different sets of information dictate different focuses in therapy.

The therapist decided to focus on Jesse and Sonny's struggle about making a connection.

Therapist: So you two were doing this funny dance—Dad's chasing Sonny, trying to be a good dad and get him interested, and you (*indicates Sonny*) figure it's all about getting your *Momma's* attention. (*Sonny looks up, nods*) So how did you respond when he came after you? You really thought he was after your Momma, right?

Sonny: I would go along but not really. In my head I was saying, I'm different from him, he's not my daddy, he don't care about me.

Th: *Did* you care about him, Jesse?

Jesse: Damn right I did! I was dying to get him to really join in and get with me, do like John done.

Sonny: (*interrupting*) That's just it! I didn't want to do like John done! He would kiss your butt and do whatever you liked, but not me.

Th: You really hate the idea of kissing anyone's butt, don't you? You're proud of being independent.

Sonny: Damn straight. Ain't nobody on earth I'll kiss their butt.

Th: So your style [clothing] these days is really a statement: "I'm my own man, separate from my father and brother"?

Sonny: Right.

Th: Did you know Dad was so frustrated and hurt that he couldn't get you more interested in him? That you wouldn't sign on with his style?

Sonny: What's he need me for? He's got John and Momma eatin' out of his hand, he don't need me.

Th: Jesse?

Jesse: I *do* need you, boy! Maybe 'cause you remind me of myself at that age, maybe 'cause I've always liked your spunkiness. . . . I don't know but it's always hurt me bad that you don't let me be a friend. I like the idea of a spunky kid—I'm spunky myself—but I don't like it that you're so disrespectful to me. I wish you'd give me a chance.

Sonny appeared moved by this invitation, in part because it included a commitment to mutual respect, and he slowly signed on to work with Jesse on establishing a different relationship.

The therapy came to focus on both men's underlying strivings: Jesse's to make a good connection with both boys as father and friend, and Sonny's to be his own man. The therapist helped Jesse to pursue Sonny directly but respectfully, teaching him that affection did not have to be controlling. Sonny slowly let himself care about Jesse and about being in the family, without feeling like he was begging for acceptance. He began to be more cooperative with them; his dress remained tough but his manner softened. Within six months, Jesse and Sonny worked together to convince the probation officer to let Sonny go on unsupervised probation.

The therapist's actions came from his belief that all the players are working on important issues behind the symptomatic front. The intake therapist got hooked on the symptoms and the least successful aspects of their transactions. He began to see their symptoms as *them*, and as all of which they were capable. The competence-oriented therapist tried to discover a healthy motivation behind the symptoms. He then used that to fuel the work necessary to alter relationships.

Searching for and finding our clients' underlying healthy striving, their competence, is a critical task in therapy. We think that it is a component of therapy that is neither explored nor emphasized enough. This book is about that search.

The Heart of a Competence Approach

The term competence was first used as a psychological variable by Robert White (1959) who focused on the importance of the striving for mastery from infancy on (see Chapter 2). We use the term competence in White's sense of inborn striving for mastery and growth. We do not intend to invoke the other common meanings of the word—adequate ability, skill acquisition, etc. We use it to reflect our belief in people's need to make their world work, to grow and change and to strive for mastery both in the external world and in their internal development.

The heart of a competence approach to therapy is four-fold: searching for people's healthy intentions embedded in their pathology; developing with them a clear vision of what they really want to master; helping them find the courage to make a proactive step in this direction; and doing this work in an atmosphere of respect and support, that is, in partnership. We will introduce each of these concepts briefly now and develop them more fully in the chapters that follow.

Healthy Intentionality

No one sets out to go on a bad journey, but many journeys end up badly. Fundamental to a competence approach is respect for people's healthy striving. There are many more healthy motives in people than we are taught to recognize. The urgency to love and be loved and to master what is put before us is universal, however distorted the presentations. It is the pursuit of those needs that keeps us going.

A healthy developmental pathway survives and wants realization in everyone, though it is sometimes hard to see. Many symptoms and behaviors that can be seen as psychopathology can also be seen as distress patterns that surround unfinished developmental business. Our work attends carefully to these healthy developmental pathways and to the potential competence undertakings that often appear in the guise of symptoms.

In almost all psychological disturbances, people's symptoms also contain healthy seeds that have developed in an unhealthy progression. A purely psychopathological orientation focuses exclusively on the distorted process and ignores the healthy impulse behind it. It takes the distortion as the important or "real" process, and sees the person as his psychopathology: "He is an obsessive compulsive," we say, as though that captures the whole person.

On the other hand, merely attending to people's strengths without recognizing and addressing their limitations and problems is also unrealistic and unhelpful. Some therapists mistakenly believe that to find and develop people's positive sides is to ignore or whitewash their inadequacies, as though we had to choose which part of a person really represents them and let the other go. A competence model suggests that we work from an integrated view:

seeing people's aspirations *and* their shortfalls; understanding their inadequacies *in light of* their hopes. We struggle to avoid the dualities that dominate western thinking—either/or, better/worse, good/bad—in order to find a more integrated and transcendent view of people.

A competence approach offers a model for integrating pathology and health. It assumes that symptoms are adaptive attempts gone awry and that the motives and passions that yield problems have a healthy side, a side of powerful striving for mastery. That striving is what needs to be understood, redirected, and harnessed for positive change. This requires of both client and therapist an understanding of the healthy roots of the problematic elements and of how they got distorted into unhealthy patterns. As White (1959) implied, people do not need to be taught how to want mastery and growth; that is innate. But to succeed, the energy that has been directed into dysfunctional behavior needs to be reoriented toward competent functioning. To reacquaint people with both their aspirations and their capabilities, one needs to approach their problems not as the enemy but as information or clues that can lead to positive growth.

Vision

One of the great deficits of most therapy is the lack of a proactive vision of what people need to move *towards* instead of a sense of what they need to move *away from*. The process of developing a map with clients of what they really want to master, however, does not simply mean constructing a prescription of the behavioral goal. To the divorced, distant father, "You can't abandon your children" is less a vision than an order. Creating a vision with clients means helping them develop an integrated redirection of their underlying motivation. Thus, helping this father remember what he truly wanted with his kids might lead to developing this kind of vision: "You experienced loss yourself as a child and, more than anything else, wanted to protect your children from that. Instead of retreating from them and their pain, teach them about your hopes for the relationship; help them to know you better."

Vision comes out of understanding the client's underlying strivings. We try to help our clients rediscover these yearnings and the energy connected with them. With that fuller understanding of themselves, they can develop a renewed sense of going after what they really want. Creating a vision has to do with helping people reconnect with their own potential; it stirs them to be genuinely interested in a different path and to reclaim parts of themselves that they have lost.

The common error in working in a positive frame such as envisioning positive change for clients, however, is the tendency to focus on the positive by ignoring the negative. Clients will feel disrespected if that occurs. Just as minimizing the impact of physical paralysis on a young woman's life seems outlandish, so also do some of the attempts by therapists to put a happy face on clients' problems. We discover people's underlying strivings by fully understanding their breakdowns as well. Believing that healthy seeds are always at the center of maladaptive patterns, we look to symptoms as information about underlying strivings. We can push people to create a different vision for themselves, to make better use of their resources, because of this real conviction that health is embedded in pathology. We try to glean from symptoms where the breakdown of developmental progress and of courage occurred and to think of how to revive both.

Courage

The third element at the heart of our approach is undertaking proactive steps that move people to go after what they really want. Some therapists see their proper role as pointing out the patterns of dysfunction: defenses, impulses, neurotic compromises. Creating that awareness in people can be very useful. It can bring unconscious patterns into consciousness, help people connect their past and their present, and offer explanations for apparently senseless behavior. It can also be an avenue through which people feel their problems and struggles are taken seriously and their pain is treated respectfully.

But this introspective, analytic process often fails to produce change. Therapy needs to be more oriented toward the direct process of helping clients take proactive steps toward better outcomes. It is not enough for clients to understand the etiology of their problems; in addition to reacting to the past, they want change in the present. And just as vision needs to be connected to the client's underlying strivings, so too proactive steps need to take the clients toward where they want to go, not where the therapist thinks they ought to go. "Stop beating your wife" is not a proactive step. On the other hand, "Let me help you find ways of getting her attention and interest that work for both of you" might be.

Helping people move toward what they really want should be a simple process, but it is not. The mental health field has failed to acknowledge how much courage it takes to move from well-oiled, maladaptive patterns to untested, healthier ones. Courage is a vital but almost entirely neglected aspect of behavior change.

In learning to think about courage, we have been aided by the work of Joseph Campbell (1990, 1988) on myth and the hero. Campbell suggested that the heroes and heroines of myth all were on a similar metaphorical quest: They went forth to "slay the dragon" (or giant, or whatever) against all odds, and succeeded. But the outcome was that they returned fundamentally changed. Campbell shows us that the dragon is a symbol of our *inner* demons, rather than mythic external ones. The hero's journey is a metaphor for the courage to undertake internal transformation. We are our own dragon, and it is ourselves and our fears and internal blocks that need slaying.

It is hard to think of the hero's journey as negative, and we are helped in this way to see the positive, competent aspects of struggle and confrontation. Campbell has said, "The hero is the one who comes to participate in life courageously and decently, in the way of nature, not in the way of personal rancor, disappointment or revenge" (1988, p. 66). This goal of a courageous, natural engagement with life guides us more than any desire to avoid the "negative" aspects of symptoms. In therapy our clients are attempting to "slay their dragons," but we often lose sight of that. We focus instead on their dysfunction, victimization, or handicap, and we become less helpful to them. Those things are not their core; their core is their desire for mastery and belonging. They become heroes when they struggle against those obstacles and move to transform their lives.

Partnership

In the Western tradition, man's struggle for transformation has typically been a solo journey. Our mythology centers on the self-determined, self-reliant individual who slays the dragon essentially alone. One of the greatest contributions of family therapy has been to emphasize interrelatedness and the circularity of life. That emphasis suggests redefining the hero's journey as an interpersonal one. It is not simply how valiantly one person can struggle, but how one makes courageous use of one's own *and others'* resources that makes us heroes.

The fourth key element of a competence approach, therefore, is partnership. Our focus becomes how we can help clients develop their vision and courage in an active partnership with us. The therapeutic relationship has always been the therapist's primary tool; we build on that premise. The focus on competence, courage, and change all take place in a collaborative context. Courage is most easily developed within a partnership characterized by caring and respect. While the therapist must have a clear map in mind, clients must trust that the movement is theirs and not the therapist's.

Healing vs. Fixing

Our use of a competence approach in therapy needs to be understood in the larger context of a healing vs. a fixing mindset. Therapeutic approaches may be divided, at the risk of some oversimplification, into healing orientations and fixing orientations. The two differ in focus, depth, usual length of treatment, and criteria of success. The core of a fixing mentality involves attention to patterns more than to people, and to the changing of those patterns. "Fixers" tend to see problems as almost entirely systemic and self-maintaining, and as responsive to even very small changes in the system's functioning. They have little interest in "individual issues" or internal distress, except for their systemic effects. Fixers see past the people to the patterns.

A healing orientation, on the other hand, looks past the patterns to the people. It sees patterns as real, but as arising out of individual distress, and tries to change patterns by changing the people who inhabit them. Growth, selfhood, and transformation are at the heart of a healing approach. The best definition of healing comes from Stephen Levine (1990): "Healing is to enter with mercy and awareness that which has been withdrawn from in judgment and hatred" (p. 4). Where a fixing approach tries to get the family out of therapy and back on the road as quickly as possible, a healing orientation is more interested in reaching people at a deeper level; healers worry less about the length of treatment and more about its depth. They go toward the symptoms, for the information and intensity they contain, rather than just trying to dispel them. Healing involves going toward what hurts and accepting it with courage, *so that it may be let go.*

The healing focus is at the core of our competence approach. Where fixing requires imagination and flexibility in order to get away from the symptoms, healing requires the competence and courage to go straight toward what is most painful and to master it. The very meaning of healing (in Levine's sense) is tied to *entering* that which has been avoided. There are many models for this in the field; it is not a new idea. Grieving, for example, requires an honest acceptance of the painful loss with all its ramifications before the healing can take place. Sexual abuse is proving to yield best to a painful but honest reclaiming of the denied, repressed, and disowned aspects of the early trauma. AA, the grandfather of successful self-help programs, relies entirely on the active acceptance of every aspect of the reality, "I am an alcoholic." There is no healing for an addict if he does not first have the courage to see the problem exactly as it is.

In spite of these models of courage and healing, the family field has most often gone in the fixing direction (Nichols, 1987). There are notable exceptions, such as Virginia Satir's work, which was deeply involved with love and courage. Perhaps the systemic focus has made it hard for us to see profound personal change as a proper focus for family therapy. Nichols (1987) has suggested that it may be that the intensity of people's personal distress scares us away. Whatever the reason, we believe that a competence focus bridges the gap between a healing focus and family work by challenging some or all members of the family to address directly and courageously the changes they need to make, individually and together, in order to regain a healthy and gratifying pathway toward the future. It helps people to reclaim the striving that they feel, but which has become part of their *dys*function, instead of part of their functioning. And it finds in people's distress the seeds of their resurgence. This requires competence, courage, and change on the part of both client and therapist. It is precisely in the revival of those elements that therapy makes a difference. That revival is what this book is about.

COMPETENCE
IN EVERYDAY LIFE

Experience is not what happens to a man. It is what a man does with what happens to him.

— Aldous Huxley

ASK SOMEONE HOW MUCH of this country's heating supply is passive solar heat. People usually answer, "Not much," thinking of places heated with passive solar technology. The true answer is close to 90%, because *all* heat is passive solar, except that small fraction that is actively generated by another source. Competence operates in the same way: It is going on all the time and fuels much of what we do, but it is usually unnoticed and unacknowledged. The underlying urge to master the environment and make the world work in a way that feels good and rewarding goes on in virtually everyone, virtually all of the time, and motivates much of our behavior.

What does competence look like in everyday life? What are the moment to moment presentations? The question can best be addressed by looking first at active *in*competence: transactions that fail. This is easier precisely because the presence of competence is so common that it is hard to see.

Everyday Transactions

Consider a series of common interactions of varying degrees of *incompetence*:

- A father wants his son to help him paint the shutters. He goes to the boy, who is absorbed in playing his guitar, and says in an angry tone of voice, "Turn off that noise and come do something useful for once."
- A child feels anxious about his parents going away on a two-night trip and leaving him with a sitter. He comes to his mother, in pain, screaming that he fell down and hurt his arm. When the mother tries to comfort him, he screams louder and pushes her away.
- A man comes home from an exhausting double shift to find his wife feeling overwhelmed by the cumulative pressure of tending their three young children. She greets him in tears. He responds, "Jesus Christ, is this what I come home to? Why do I bother to come home?"
- An adolescent wanting to use her parents' car approaches her parents with the statement, "Do you realize that I *never* get *anything* I want in this place?"
- A wife wanting affection and reassurance from her husband mopes around the house, hoping he'll notice. He doesn't. She goes to bed early without telling him why.
- A ten-year-old, hoping to be invited into a ball game, stands on the sidelines for an hour. When one of the boys playing finally asks him what he wants, he says, "Nothing."

Each of these scenarios makes us cringe, as we watch people hinder their own success by undermining the relationships that could help them. Each scenario looks "pathological," in that the behavior is maladaptive. The motives, however, are healthy and understandable. In every one of these examples there is an incompetent reaction in the sense that people do something that actively makes their situation worse. They get further from what they want rather than closer to it. They misuse both internal and external resources.

It is not hard to imagine each scenario playing out in a different way: the father asks his son to help in an effective way, or the husband commiserates with his wife's distress and she feels relieved and comforted. It is also not hard to imagine that the next step of the sequence might be quite different: the son agrees to help; the wife relaxes and then responds to her husband's needs, etc. We know that these chains of interactions tend to be self-perpetuating, in either direction. Compare those failed transactions to the examples that follow.

- A one-year-old coos to get her mother's attention. The mother responds by picking her up.
- A three-year-old gets his parents to help him approach and pat a feared dog.
- A seven-year-old, wanting her parent's approval, works hard in school, does well, and gets praised and appreciated.
- A ten-year-old, hungry for candy, sweet-talks his mother into taking him along with her on an errand, and then playfully cons her into treating him to a candy bar. They both get pleasure out of the interaction.
- A teenage boy, hoping a girl will take an interest in him, joins the singing group she is in and does well. She notices him, is impressed with his singing, and they strike up an acquaintance.
- A 15-year-old girl, wanting to establish her independence, gets a radical hair cut and a nose ring without asking. She accepts the grounding that follows with minimal complaint.
- A young husband, eager to mend fences with his new wife, sends her flowers the day after a fight and calls her office to leave a cryptic love message.

Transactions that work are transactions that help a person get what he or she wants in a developmentally healthy way. A transaction works when a person knows what he or she wants (more or less), does something appropriate (more or less) to try to get it, and succeeds (more or less).

The examples above may sound trivial, but they are not. Each one involves a considerable degree of knowing what is wanted, having some idea of how to get it, and executing the plan. All of these are complex tasks. Think how easily most of these examples could have gone wrong. The seven-year-old wants her parents approval but merely hopes she'll get it, instead of working hard in school; the boy joins the choir but spends all of his time showing off instead of singing, thereby repelling the girl; the repentant husband can't apologize outright and takes another subtle swipe at the wife even as he approaches her. The possibilities are endless for misfires in all aspects of transactions.

It is instructive to examine the difference between the transactions that work and those that do not. There is often only a slight nuance of difference between the two. Many unsuccessful interactions come amazingly close to being competent and effective, and vice versa. One similarity between the two, however, is that both tend to produce more of their own kind. The adolescent who says to his parents "I never get anything I want" as a way of trying to get his hands on the car is very apt to induce in them an angry, withholding response on the order of, "If that's how you feel, then fine. You *won't* get what you want." Nobody feels good about the transaction, no one gains, and presumably no one gets what they most want out of it.

Conversely, in the competent direction, there are multiple gains. The boy who joins the choral group to make contact with the admired girl experiences the pleasure of performing well in multiple spheres (singing, group acceptance, catching the girl's eye, etc.). His competent functioning is apt to induce the girl to respond in kind and to create the sort of contact that gets him what he wants. In both kinds of functioning, the path is laid down for more of the same, and each breeds its own natural aftermath.

The most striking difference between effective and ineffective transactions is the nature of the individual's use of self. In the competent undertakings, people typically make a straightforward, active engagement with what they want. They go after their goal fairly directly and put themselves into it. There is a measure of courage and heart in each of those transactions. There is also wisdom; wisdom is choosing a goal that is attainable and developmentally on track.

By contrast, the unsuccessful transactions typically involve indirect and partially dishonest pursuit of the goal. The people protect themselves, rather than behaving vulnerably, as they try to bring something about without putting themselves on the line. There is a powerful impact to the straightforward and direct presentation of self, and it is partly definitional of competence. As we have studied competent undertakings of all kinds, we repeatedly find them characterized by honesty, courage, and an active engagement with both the issue and the other players. The refusal to back off from the desired goal has much to do with getting what we want and need.

The Underpinnings of Competence

The term competence is an imperfect one that we have struggled with because of its varied meanings and connotations. We have stuck with it for two reasons: There are no good alternatives, and its pedigree is ideal. Robert White developed the notion of competence in the 1950s in very much the spirit that our work has developed. White's central focus on the human desire to master and enjoy the environment and people's desire to connect day-to-day activity with deeper motives and issues are the spiritual as well as the academic forebears of our work. Let us begin with a review of the concept of competence and then develop a new focus for it that will carry through our work.

"Motivation Reconsidered"

White's seminal paper, "Motivation Reconsidered: The Concept of Competence," appeared in 1959, although it was not the first work to take up the idea of an innate motivation to master the environment. Hendrick had written years earlier of "an inborn drive to do and to learn how to do" (1942, p. 35). He developed the idea that, contrary to psychoanalytic principles, there was an "instinct to master" the environment, which yielded "primary pleasure" where an action "enables the individual to control and alter his environment" (p. 36). White built on this and, with others in psychology, challenged the idea that only the Freudian drives of sex and aggression affected behavior. The Freudian belief depended heavily on the idea that behavior arose from biologically based drives. Psychoanalysis roundly rejected the idea that the individual could be motivated by something as ethereal and cerebral as mastery or control.

White introduced two important concepts. First he showed the extensive impact of competence from birth. He defined that impact as "an organism's capacity to interact effectively with its environment" (p. 297). Drawing on animal studies and child development research, White highlighted the innate interest of the organism in mastering its surroundings and controlling its environment. He wrote of the importance of "action systems and the consequences of action" (p. 311) as having a major impact in the development of the ego.

This idea, too, was heretical—that the individual developed from the outside in, as well as from the inside out. This view represented a bold departure from the narrow confines of psychoanalytic theory. Where Freud had tied virtually all functioning to the two primary drives (sex and aggression) and a complex set of derivatives, White added the crucial element of the individual's "intrinsic need to deal with the environment" (p. 318). He focused on the importance and the effect of behavior, interaction, and cognitive mastery on the development of the human spirit and personality.

"The Feeling of Efficacy"

In addition to recognizing and delineating the ways that competent behavior or mastery shows up and is important in people's development, White also postulated the existence of an *underlying competence motivation*. He distinguished between mastery for mastery's sake—a purely behavioral habit of mastery acquired because of the reinforcement involved—and an intrinsic motivation he called "effectance motivation." White felt that this condition " . . . aims for the *feeling of efficacy*, not the vitally important learnings that come as its consequence" (p. 323, italics added).

By a "feeling of efficacy," we take White to mean a cumulative feeling learned from experiencing competence over time, the feeling of pleasure in the confidence that one is able to make the world work. The awareness that a person can have an impact on her environment and make happen what she wants or needs to happen is powerful. It is not a sense of omnipotence; it is a sense of trust in the manageability of the world and of hope for one's ability to have an effect.

The feeling of efficacy develops out of experiences with competent undertakings. Very early on, the infant, given responsive caretakers, begins to be aware of his capacity to make things happen. He cries and someone picks him up; she vocalizes and someone vocalizes back. The infant who repetitively drops her spoon from the high chair may enjoy the noise or the excitement, but primarily she is experimenting with making something happen. She is creating a response and having an effect on her environment. Responsive caretakers are important, in part, for their contributions to this awareness and to the ongoing development of a sense of efficacy.

Having a desired and effective impact leads, in time, to a positive overall sense of one's power in and control over the world. The sense of efficacy produces hope because it reduces the sense of powerlessness and makes the future seem more manageable. It is a powerful determinant of both self concept and behavior; its absence is equally so in the negative direction.

Contributions from Research

Since White's work, competence has been studied as a major variable in development and in mental health by a number of investigators. In a recent review article, Masterpasqua (1991) suggested that " . . . the epigenesis of competence serves as the motor for individual development as well as for continuing adaptation of the species" (p. 1367). He sees competence as "a major unifying force within psychology" and shows how competence or a lack of it is a more accurate predictor of maladjustment than the presence of symptoms (p. 1370). While we often use the concept of competence differently than researchers do, we entirely agree with Masterpasqua that "[w]hat is most predictive of mental health is the appraisal we make of our capacity to deal with major and minor life events" (p. 1369). It is not innate pathology or even innate ability, but our *sense of our ability* to master problems that determines how we turn out.

Bandura's (1990) review of the research reaches a similar conclusion: "Thus, individuals who believe themselves to be inefficacious are likely to effect little change even in environments that provide many opportunities. Conversely, those who have a strong sense of efficacy, through ingenuity and perseverance, figure out ways of exercising some measure of control in environments containing limited opportunities and many constraints" (pp. 337–8). Bandura (1990) notes further that the accuracy of self-appraisal of one's efficacy is not critical. In fact, so-called normals distort reality much more than people who have been identified as depressed or anxious. Bandura (1990) cites research that suggests that depressed people tend to be realistic in their self-appraisal; non-depressed people view themselves more competently than they really are. Thus, it appears to matter less how accurate your sense of competency is than that you have a sense of competency.

Several other research inquiries into competence have been helpful to us as we have worked to apply the concept to therapy. A brief and very selective review of these follows. Each one highlights an important aspect of competence that might otherwise escape attention.

Competence and Attachment

One way of understanding how the sense of competence begins comes from the research of Sroufe (1983, 1978), who has studied competence from the point of view of its connection to attachment. He concluded that babies who were "assessed as secure in their attachment as infants were much more enthusiastic and persistent and showed more positive feelings than did children who had earlier been assessed as anxiously attached" (1978, p. 55). In his studies, securely attached children rated higher than the others on 11 of the 13 measures of competence. The presence of a secure attachment figure seems to make it possible for children to explore and deal with the world, confident that a safe harbor is nearby. "Even when floundering," Sroufe writes, "[S]ome children may not lose their sense that they can affect the environment and that they will be all right" (1978, p. 55). For adults as well, that sense is crucial to working effectively in the world. It is the basis for acting positively and doing what one can to affect one's world. At its extreme, the alternative sense is the "learned helplessness" syndrome that characterizes depression (Seligman, 1975). When a person has little or no belief that he can do anything that will make a difference, he gives up in the face of difficulty. Sroufe's work ties the presence or absence of such a feeling directly to the caregiver-child bond:

> Through the sensitive interaction the infant learns that he can have an impact on the world and that stimulation in the presence of the caregiver is not threatening. In the presence of the caregiver he can tolerate the excitement of new experiences because he has learned that the caregiver is available when needed. Ultimately, the baby comes to believe that such resources lie within himself, and he develops a sense of trust in his caregiver. This trust eventually becomes a belief in his own competence. (1978, p. 57)

Sroufe concludes that, "Competence in early years does not guarantee competence in later life. But it is a good start" (1978, p. 57). He states clearly, however, that it is not just an early-childhood-or-never proposition; later experience with learning to manage difficult stimuli effectively is as important as early experience. How children get started is important, but learning to manage competently is crucial whenever it occurs because it gives the individual some control over his environment and some hope for the future. We believe that Sroufe's idea that competence is learned in the context of a good relationship extends to later learning as well. The various contributions of helpers—caregiver with baby, parent with child, teacher with student, or therapist with client—make an important difference at all ages. The competence-seeking individual often needs a person to help her learn a sense of efficacy in the context of a relationship. Whether it is parent, teacher, friend, or therapist, the interpersonal aspect of competence development is an important one throughout the life cycle.

Competence Skills

Strayhorn's work, delineated in his book, *The Competent Child* (1988), has also influenced our thinking about competence. Though his slant on competence is more oriented towards "skills," the skills Strayhorn delineates are not simple behavioral goals. Rather, he has developed a complex and full compilation of the actual behaviors *and attitudes* that make life work. Strayhorn has been particularly interested in what people derived from psychotherapy that helps them. The 59 items he calls the "Psychological Health Skills Axis" (Table 1) involve complex integrations of cognitive, emotional, and behavioral abilities, which promote healthy development and are learnable in psychotherapy. While the skills format tends to oversimplify the great complexity of these items, they are still recognizable as the factors by which we manage our lives effectively. The absence of very many of them seriously reduces the individual's capacity to manage some necessary aspects of life.

Several things are worth noting about Strayhorn's list. First, he has left out very little; it is difficult to think of a strength that is not represented on his axis. It is therefore helpful in breaking the vast heading of "competence" down into its component parts. Second, his structure is fundamentally developmental; the nine categories roughly correspond to levels of increasing autonomy and self-actualization. They also go from the most fundamental issues (attachment, separation) toward the more elective (relaxing, organizing). Third, his skills are heavily interpersonal. He does not eschew the complexity of interpersonal events for the false simplicity of behavioral events. In all these ways, Strayhorn's work is helpful and thought-provoking. Where Sroufe helps us consider how competence gets built on an interpersonal foundation, Strayhorn helps us see the nature of what we must learn to do in order to keep developing in a healthy direction.

Sroufe's and Strayhorn's work complement one another by addressing how competence develops and what it consists of in an ideal sense. But, given that none of us have ideal bases in secure attachment nor all of the skills we need to develop optimally, how do we manage? How do we grow and keep moving toward more competent functioning? Why do we not give up?

TABLE 1 Psychological Health Skills Axis

***

Group 1: Closeness, trusting, relationship building
 1. Accurately assessing the trustworthiness of another person, and trusting when appropriate.
 2. Accepting help, being dependent without shame, asking for help appropriately.
 3. Tolerating and enjoying sustained closeness, attachment, and commitment of another.
 4. Intimately disclosing and revealing oneself to another in a situation where it is safe.
 5. Nurturing someone else: being kind and helpful.
 6. Nurturing oneself: delivering assuring or caretaking cognitions to oneself, and feeling comforted by such cognitions.
 7. Expressing gratitude, admiration, and other positive feelings toward others.
 8. Initiating social contacts appropriately; getting attention from others in appropriate ways.
 9. Engaging in social conversation.
10. Listening, empathizing, encouraging another to disclose.

Group 2: Handling separation and independence
11. Making decisions independently; carrying out actions independently.
12. Tolerating separation from close others.
13. Handling rejection.
14. Dealing with disapproval, criticism, and lack of respect from others.
15. Having a good time by oneself; tolerating aloneness, tolerating not getting someone's attention.

Group 3: Handling joint decisions and interpersonal conflict
16. Dealing with someone's doing or wanting something that conflicts with one's own preferences; deciding how much self-sacrifice, assertion, conciliation, forgiveness, giving behavior, resignation, and/or punishment constitutes the best response.
17. Generating creative options for solutions to interpersonal problems.
18. Recognizing and choosing reasonable solutions to interpersonal problems.
19. Negotiating: talking out conflicts and reaching joint decisions (includes the subskills of being persuasive, using tact, using well-chosen timing, and discerning and explaining the reasons for disagreement).
20. Assertion and dominance skills: sticking up for one's own welfare, taking charge, enjoying winning a competition, exerting one's will over others when appropriate, resisting inappropriate influence.
21. Conciliation and submission skills: giving in, conceding a point, tolerating losing a competition, admitting one was wrong, allowing oneself to be led, allowing another's will to dominate when appropriate.
22. Recognizing and praising the portion of another's behavior that is positive.
23. Tolerating, without needing to control or direct, a wide range of other people's behavior.
24. Forgiving other people, being able to relinquish anger.

Group 4: Dealing with frustration and unfavorable events
25. Handling frustration, tolerating adverse circumstances.
26. Handling one's own mistakes and failures.
27. Tolerating a second person's getting something that one wants for oneself; avoiding inappropriately large jealousy.
28. Correctly estimating the danger of situations; being relatively fearless in relatively nondangerous situations.
29. Feeling appropriate fear when danger is present.
30. Feeling appropriate guilt when one has harmed others.
31. Tolerating one's own feelings — including painful feelings — without making matters worse by fearing them, feeling guilty over them, not permitting oneself any feelings, or otherwise overestimating the danger of the feeling.
32. Tolerating thoughts, impulses, or fantasies that must not be acted on, with confidence that idea and actions are not the same; tolerating less than 100% control of these mental events.

(continued)

TABLE 1 (Continued)

___

Group 5: Celebrating good things, feeling pleasure
33. Enjoying approval, compliments, and other positive attention from others.
34. Celebrating and internally rewarding oneself for one's own accomplishments and successes.
35. Feeling pleasure from doing kind, loving acts for others.
36. Enjoying discovery, taking pleasure from exploration.
37. Feeling gratitude for what others have done.
38. Celebrating and feeling the blessings of luck or fate.
39. Enjoying physical affection without various fears interfering.
40. Having romantic or erotic feelings attached to desirable stimulus situations.

Group 6: Working for delayed gratification
41. Denying oneself present gratification for the sake of future gain.
42. Complying, obeying; submitting to reasonable authority.
43. Concentrating on, maintaining attention to, and persisting on tasks.
44. Maintaining healthy habits regarding drinking, smoking, drug use, exercise, and diet.
45. Being honest and dependable when it is difficult to be so.
46. Developing competences that bring approval and acceptance from people: (a) work-related, (b) school-related, (c) recreational.
47. Forgoing consumption in favor of saving; financial delay of gratification.

Group 7: Relaxing, playing
48. Relaxing; letting the mind drift and the body be at ease.
49. Playing, becoming childlike, experiencing glee, being spontaneous.
50. Enjoying humor; finding and producing comedy in life.

Group 8: Cognitive processing through words, symbols, and images
51. Using words to conceptualize the world: verbal skills.
52. Recognizing and being able to verbalize one's own feelings.
53. Correctly assessing other people's feelings; seeing things from the other's point of view (including the impact of one's behavior on others).
54. Accurately assessing the degree of control one has over specific events.
55. Decision making: defining a problem, gathering information, generating options, predicting and evaluating consequences, making a choice.
56. Thinking before acting; letting thoughts mediate between situation and action.
57. Being organized and planful in the use of time, money, and physical objects: deciding upon priorities, consciously deciding upon and organizing allocations, carrying out those decisions.
58. Accurately assessing one's own skills and abilities in various times, tasks, and circumstances.
59. Accurately assessing the skills and character of others, based upon evidence rather than upon prejudice, overgeneralization, wish-fulfilling fantasies, or other distortions.
60. Being able to use imagination and fantasy as a tool in rehearsing or evaluating a plan, or adjusting to an event or situation.

Group 9: An adaptive sense of direction and purpose
61. Aiming toward making circumstances better, in the long run, rather than worse; seeking reward and not punishment.
62. Assigning to activity a "meaning" or "purpose" that allows effort to provide a sense of fulfillment (even in unpleasant circumstances).

From J. Strayhorn (1988) The competent child: An approach to psychotherapy and preventive mental health. New York: Guilford, pp. 28–29. Reprinted with permission.

"Resilience"

Here, the work of Michael Rutter (1987) is instructive. Rutter investigated the component of competence that he calls resilience—"the positive role of individual differences in people's responses to stress and adversity" (1987, p. 316). Rutter studied people who develop competence under very adverse circumstances and who "manage to maintain high self-esteem and self-efficacy in spite of facing the same adversities that lead other people to give up and lose hope" (1987, p. 317). Rutter describes several key elements of this process. It is not *avoidance* of risk, he says, but successful engagement with it that leads to a sense of competence. ("Life is not a matter of holding good cards, but of playing a poor hand well," as Robert Louis Stevenson said.) Rutter also found that the ability to maintain competent functioning in adverse circumstances is often a turning point in a person's life that "then determines the direction of trajectory for years to follow" (p. 318). In other words, success begets success because it changes how people see themselves. The process reminds one of Campbell's description of heroes as returning fundamentally changed. Rutter also found that resilience is made up of many factors, from effective planning to strong interpersonal relationships to the chance occurrence of stress factors. It is not a simple commodity, but a complex group of abilities that also depends to some extent on luck.

Rutter reduces to four the main components of resilience: (1) the reduction of risk impact (controlling how much stress one is exposed to); (2) the reduction of negative chain reactions (learning how to minimize the damage rather than add insult to injury); (3) the sense of self-esteem and self-efficacy (internal resources that allow the individual to feel lovable and capable in spite of difficult events); and (4) the opening up of opportunities (taking advantage of possibilities). Interestingly, Rutter ties self-esteem and self-efficacy to two types of experiences: secure love relationships (see Sroufe) and the successful accomplishment of important tasks (see Strayhorn).

In an important way, Rutter shows that it is precisely in how we handle the difficult turning points in our lives that we grow and change. Developing resilience to some extent occurs naturally, but can also be learned, shaped, and maximized. How to use therapy to help people develop a sense of resilience is of major interest to us.

Two Kinds of Mothering

A final research finding that is helpful in clarifying the potential application of competence to therapy is that of Scheinfeld (1983). He investigated the difference between families that produce competent children (as measured by school performance) and those that do not. Using a group of lower-income black families in inner-city Chicago, Scheinfeld found that the success of boys in school correlated strongly with two very different modes of mother-child interaction. Mothers of achieving sons had what Scheinfeld called "appetitive adaptive aim; i.e., the parent wanted the child to be striving toward experiences of personal meaning, satisfaction and pleasure as ends in themselves" (p. 129). These mothers demonstrated a strong interest in and support for what Scheinfeld termed "active engagement" with the world. This came in the form of several specific competencies, each operationally defined and measured, that these mothers both modeled and encouraged: purposefulness, trust, social connectedness, active exchange with the environment beyond the home, development of interpersonal skills, a capacity for effective relating to authority, and concern with emotional needs. This list covers a variety of abilities that are characteristic of a competent child. The effective mothers in Scheinfeld's study expressed and acted on those values.

"By contrast," Scheinfeld states, "The adaptive aim held for their children by the parents of low achievers tended to be an aversive one; i.e., the aim was to avoid outcomes experienced as negative by the child or by the parent" (p. 129). These mothers demonstrated a pattern he called "defensive isolation" from the world, in the form of "ideals that emphasize constraint, isolation and adult control" (p. 127). Where active engagement mothers supported competence-gaining activity, defensive isolation mothers supported and modeled adaptation to threat. They saw the world as something dangerous and to be avoided.

The correlations between these styles and boys' achievement were highly significant. Mothers of the low achievers seemed to "ignore or negate the importance of the boys' own interests, motives or emotional needs and place an emphasis both on isolation from the environment and on external control by adults" (p. 138). These mothers had no model of competence-gaining activity or active engagement with the environment. Instead, they saw the world as hostile, and most involvement with it as doomed to failure.

This study, while only partially successful in its methodology and completeness, gives a strong view of two very different child-rearing styles. Scheinfeld credits one pattern of mothering (and probably fathering, too, though he did not include fathers in his statistical analysis for reasons of underrepresentation) with teaching and reinforcing a positive, proactive model of interaction with the world. In any case, parents' own experiences of the world and proclivity to expect life to be enjoyable or defeating are passed on to their children.

Perhaps the most crucial aspect of Scheinfeld's study for our own purposes is his focus on the general outlook of the family. Scheinfeld's description of "striving toward experiences of personal meaning, satisfaction and pleasure" (p. 129) is an eloquent statement of what we mean by and experience as the sense of competence. Like White's idea of a feeling of efficacy, it is a sense of wanting and being capable of achieving mastery in one's world. When that sense of either wanting or believing in the possibility of reaching those goals is lost, valuable hope, striving, and energy are lost with it.

Beyond the sense of possibility, Scheinfeld's study also seems to relate strongly to the ethics of therapy. Much therapy with a psychopathological focus runs the risk of emulating the "defensive isolation" position: "to avoid outcomes experienced as negative by the child or the parent." If therapy is built primarily around what that client did wrong and what his or her tendency to malfunction may be (that is, what to move *away from*), it is more apt to produce a self-inhibiting person who will try to avoid problems. A competence orientation is more apt to produce "striving toward experiences of personal meaning," the "active engagement" that the more successful families modeled. While this extrapolation from Scheinfeld to therapy has been simplified, it does emphasize the important difference between a method of therapy that fundamentally turns on restraint and controlling one's illness vs. one that is centered on proactive striving. Both foci are real and important, but therapy has largely lacked the latter focus over the years.

A Working Definition

In addition to the concepts presented, there are many others that have come from the study of competence (cf. Sternberg and Kolligian, 1990). Similarly, there are many variations in the definition of competence. We have quite a precise intention in using the term, but it is a little like using "love" or "anger" — people will associate their own meaning. Accordingly, we wish to spell out more fully the definition of competence we use and break it down into several parts.

The best definition of competence for our purposes is supplied by Waters and Sroufe: "The competent individual is one who is able to make use of environmental and personal resources to achieve a good developmental outcome" (1983, p. 81). This definition implies several very important aspects of the term as we use it. First, the definition implies an active, integrative *process*: making use of resources of several kinds with larger goals in mind. Thus it is different from a simple skill one can possess and use. As delineated previously, we see it as a mindset that *involves both motivation and action* designed to deal effectively with the problems life puts in one's way.

Secondly, Waters and Sroufe make direct reference to the *active* nature of competence ("able to make use of . . . "). It is a force to be used, not a qualification to be owned (as in, "He is a competent speller."). Thirdly, it includes being able to use both personal and environmental resources; to waste either one limits competence significantly. Maintaining a healthy balance of inner and outer resources is one of life's most useful abilities.

Finally, the definition emphasizes developmental progress as a basic criterion of competence. This again takes it out of the realm of a commodity and reminds us that an undertaking is only competent if it is congruent with appropriate developmental needs. For a child of five to crawl into his mother's lap when frightened may be a competent undertaking, while for a 15-year-old to do so is not. This definition thus implies a definite, if mild, value orientation, which precludes the immature or unhealthy use of resources. It is not just coping with, or managing, but *mastering* difficulties, and their internal referents, that constitutes competence.

One of the reasons we borrow Waters and Sroufe's definition is that it emphasizes active, integrative use of internal and external resources for a developmentally healthy result in response to challenge. We include among people's potential resources energy that has become embedded in their pathology. It is the underlying desire for mastery and belonging to which we are drawn. While the specifics of any competent undertaking are of interest, it is not the actions but the *spirit* of competence that is of primary concern. Waters and Sroufe (1983) reiterate that competence is " . . . identified with the ability to mobilize and coordinate these resources in such a way that opportunities are created and the potentials or resources in the environment are realized; again, for a good developmental outcome" (p. 63). Our synthesis of Waters and Sroufe's ideas is this: *Competence is the capacity to use everything you have, including the energy that drives symptoms and problems, to realize your deepest and best strivings.* It is less a matter of possessing skills than of developing a sense of your inherent capacity to move forward in a healthy manner, whatever the challenges.

The ways that life presents both challenges and the resources to meet those challenges effectively are interesting and varied. An unusual version of it was made apparent to one of us [Waters] in a case he was seeing. It reminds us that most competence occurs in everyday life, without the contribution of our therapeutic expertise.

"The Wild One"   Mike, a 16-year-old boy I had been seeing for several months, was in a downward spiral of bad behavior. Mike's performance was marginal in school and society, and he continued to act out his sense of uselessness. He had been an occasional drinker and thief but was beginning to actively choose both. I was not making a dent as I tried to help him look at his inner life and get a grip on what he wanted.

Then his Uncle Mario came to town. His father's brother, last heard from eight years ago and unknown to Mike, arrived unannounced one evening on a Harley-Davidson chopper. Long haired and bearded, he looked like the devil to Mike's parents, and God incarnate to Mike. He moved in "for a few days" and became a magnet for Mike. In the process of making substantial repairs to his motorcycle (part of the reason for the visit), he taught Mike how the bike worked and took him everywhere on it. The parents were panicked, but I was picking up some clues for our work. Mike reported to me that when he had complained about having to go see me for therapy, his uncle had dressed him down directly. "I could have used some of that stuff," he quoted his uncle as saying. "I spent *years* digging out of the hole I got into because I didn't have it." With Uncle Mario's endorsement, Mike found our sessions more interesting.

And I *still* didn't make a dent. But Uncle Mario did. He was diligent about his bike, direct in his communication, helpful in his brother's household, and straight as an arrow. He not only didn't drink, he went religiously to AA meetings and worked his program. He even "made amends" to his brother for bad treatment over his years of alcohol and substance abuse, in Mike's presence. He looked like an outlaw, but he had a powerful internal compass at work. Mike loved both features.

Mike's identification with Uncle Mario produced a dramatic change. He stopped drinking and got a job to make it possible to get a car—or a bike, he wasn't sure. He went to AA meetings occasionally with Mario and started talking to me more honestly about his own experiences and feelings. Through Mario's example, he saw a path out of the mess he was in. Once he had somewhere to go *to*, he could begin to look at where he was stuck.

I didn't have a voice that Mike was willing to learn from; Mario did, and he came at a good time. In a few months, Mike went from a lost soul to a recovering soul. He was lucky (as was I) that Mario came along and stirred up an entirely different part of him. Long after Mario left (though he returned periodically), Mike stayed attached to this part of himself, to the way of being that Mario helped him discover. I had not known how to get that part of Mike going at all; I did know enough to make room for Mario and to support Mike's interest in him.

It was quite clear in this case that Mario's good influence did not depend on the therapist's presence. The transformation would have occurred just as well without the therapy. Mario was an angel put in Mike's path, and Mike made good use of him. It is not uncommon in life that an unexpected boon appears; the challenge is to make use of it. Credit Mario for providing Mike with a highly engaging alternative path. Credit Mike for taking it, sticking with it, and learning to love it. Credit the therapist for staying out of their way. Learning to recognize and make use of angels is a vital form of competence.

Competence is everywhere. It is the passive solar heat of psychological growth. It is in parents and caregivers, in school and society; it is even available in crisis and challenge. Most centrally and importantly, it is in us. It is an inherent motivation of the greatest power, which will emerge if given a chance (and sometimes some help). The experience of it is rewarding and self-reinforcing, not just for what it produces but for the inner experience of feeling competent. We all inherently know the power of mastery, from personal experience and observation. When it works it is wonderful; when it is absent it is painful. The question then becomes, how do we maximize its presence in therapy?

three

COMPETENCE IN THERAPY

Do not oppose forces, use them: God is a verb, not a noun.

—Buckminster Fuller

THE IDEA OF COMPETENCE is the centerpiece of our way of thinking because it is fundamental to change. In our experience, people make changes in their lives when they feel *able* to change. People feel strong enough to take that risk when they are aware of their own capabilities and feel supported in that strength. Change does not come from a clear understanding of our failings, but from some sense of being able to master and transcend them. While that sense usually includes understanding what those failures are, it is the feeling of capability to transcend them, and not merely the understanding, that potentiates change.

Put another way, a proactive process of moving toward change occurs when people feel competent, have a vision, and are courageous. Competence is knowing how to move and having a sense of one's ability to do so effectively. Vision is knowing where you want to go. Courage is willingness to take the leap, try the change, test one's ability. Together these are the elements of change.

Competence is the basic element. To move forward, we must have some sense of our ability to master what lies ahead of us. As we develop that sense, we become increasingly capable of proceeding. Like the baby who tests the world around him carefully before he ventures out, or the rock climber who gets more adventurous as he learns the individual moves and maneuvers, we build our courage out of what we have mastered. A sense of competence and knowing how to do something increases our appetite for more challenge and our willingness to risk. In that way competence is the basic protein of courage and of change. Whatever we are able to do in the way of growth and self-actualization generally occurs in small steps of increased competence.

The question then becomes one of bringing our clients' competence to life in therapy. What are the steps involved in, and the thinking behind, structuring therapy around the development of competence? In this chapter we will take up that question. But, as before, it helps to look first at the patterns that have *not* worked well in order to get a clearer focus on what will.

Common Errors in Therapy

There are three kinds of errors that dominate ineffective therapy and make it unhelpful or at least less helpful and powerful than it might otherwise be. The first error is a lack of theme and focus. When this occurs therapy has no center. Therapy needs to have a focus, a thematic heart that recurs and occupies a central place in the family's awareness. It is that theme and core that keeps therapy coherent. Without it, therapy wanders vaguely, with the therapist following whatever thread the family makes apparent. Peripheral threads often need exploring, but to be useful they must be tied back in to a larger formulation.

Another way of saying this is that therapist and client must have a vision of where the client wants to go. That vision helps organize the data and enables the therapist to determine what issues need to be focused on and what ones held aside. Therapy must be centered and forward-looking. We have a loose rule of thumb that helps our trainees think about this. We say that if we, as supervisors, should meet a trainee's family outside of the clinic and ask them, "What are you working on in family therapy?" they should be able to answer with some general accuracy. If their answer is, "We talk about whatever problem comes up," then the therapist either does not have a core focus or has not articulated it clearly enough for the family.

A related problem is having a focus that is too general or vague. "Better communication," for example, is never an acceptable goal of therapy. Everyone could benefit from better communication; it is more or less like citing "improved mental health" as a core goal. The therapist needs a stronger, clearer goal. Better communication by itself is an insufficient theme that does not adequately focus the work.

The second general error that undermines good therapy occurs when there is a strong theme and focus, but no push for change. This typically occurs when the focus is mostly or entirely retrospective and pathology based. Families and, to an even greater extent, couples can get in a retrospective loop that actually mires them in the past and in the problems in a way that impedes change. Not all pathology focused therapy falls under this heading, of course; it is common for awareness of past patterns and failures to lead to changed behavior and improved functioning in the present. But such progress is not guaranteed, and unfortunately it is quite common for therapists to hold to a strong retrospective core that contains a good map of the prison, but no route for the escape.

The third common error that renders therapy less useful is the reverse of this last error. Instead of abundant insight but no change, sometimes therapy produces change, but of a type that is not integral to the people involved. Behavioral, paradoxical, or purely cognitive changes can be made, which alter the life space of the person *but not the person himself*. It is possible to alter sequences of interaction or patterns of reinforcement or communication without reaching the person or engaging him in any way that empowers him or affects his sense of and use of self. Altered sequences can do little to develop people's emotional connection with one another unless the change comes from inside. The goal of therapy is not merely symptom relief, it is also to directly enhance clients' sense of efficacy. In order to do this, they must feel the change is emanating from within them.

These three errors are the major ones we try to redress with our focus on competence. We are trying to maximize the possibility of therapy based on a strong internal focus that yields movement toward positive change. Movement is the key, but not movement per se. We specifically seek movement with a clear inner referent and a powerful personal theme. When movement is tied in to the person and evolves from a real commitment to change, it is very different from movement for movement's sake.

Four Components

Moving to a more effective way of working in therapy requires more specific guidelines. While a competence approach is hardly a "cookbook" formulaic method, we have found the following elements, cited in Chapter 1, particularly important. These are not new concepts, but they require clarification and emphasis as the primary elements of our approach.

1. Understand the Pathology and Underlying Strivings

When we accept and understand someone's pathological behavior, its present manifestations and the purposes it served at conception, the healthy impulse hidden inside it can be found, nurtured, and developed. This frees people from the shame of their pathology and provides them the opportunity to use it as a primary source of information and energy. Often this involves specifically turning the symptom on its head and reincorporating the "negative" of the symptom as "positive" evidence of the healthy striving. For example, to find the need for success that is masked by overcontrolling behavior or the appropriate anger that fuels rebellion can dramatically change people's sense of where they need to go.

"Close Friends"   A very anxious, somewhat obsessive-compulsive 14-year-old girl was brought to a therapist by her equally anxious parents. Among other symptoms, they were deeply worried because she talked at length to her hamster. She showed no interest in her peers, only in this hamster. The therapist was respectful of this and asked how she had chosen the hamster. "He

listens," the girl replied. The therapist asked the girl to bring the hamster to the next (individual) session. The girl complied, with a mixture of anxiety and real enthusiasm. The therapist let the girl steer the session and introduce the hamster. As the girl stroked and handled the hamster, the therapist could see her relax, open up, and stop attending to the compulsive concerns that usually preoccupied her. She became warmer, clearly liking the therapist's appreciation and understanding of her odd relationship with the animal.

The therapist let the girl teach her how to talk to the animal correctly. By letting the girl display her own ability, the bond between therapist and client was strengthened; and the therapist absorbed some of the hamster's luster. She developed a reputation with the girl as "*another* good listener" and, as such, was entrusted with the girl's fears of inadequacy and unlovableness, which were fueling the obsessional behavior. By recognizing in the girl's relationship with the hamster an underlying striving for connection as well as her great fear of attempting that with people, the therapist was able to make a connection with her. Neither the dysfunction nor the healthy striving needed to be discounted.

2. Develop a Vision

Developing a vision with the client of where he or the family wants or needs to go is a critical component of a competence-based approach to therapy. The vision of what clients want to be doing instead of their dysfunction follows naturally when you have reoriented them to their healthy underlying strivings. Once a vision is established it is easier to determine the steps for getting there.

"Gruff and Ready"   A poor, dysfunctional, and sad-looking family appeared at our clinic because of their social worker's concern about father's ability to parent. The gruff, bear-like father terrorized the family with his angry demeanor and his tendency to control the three boys (10, 8, 4) by physical threats. He would raise the back of his hand and yell, "Shut up!" and they would freeze and cringe. Everyone agreed that he almost never actually hit anyone, but fear that he might was rampant. The therapist said to him, "You really want them to obey, don't you?" Father concurred, "I want them to be good boys. I want this to be a

good family." The therapist pushed further, "What else would you like?" Father paused, then said haltingly, "Well I want them to love me, too. I hated my daddy, and I don't want that." "Good," said the therapist, "And what have you taught them about that? I can see you've taught them to freeze, but what have you taught them about how to get a hug from you?" Father allowed that he knew very little about that and wouldn't know where to begin. The therapist supported the father and slowly helped him develop a way he could induce and enjoy hugs from his sons. Father was not only very proud of himself for this, he was hooked on therapy and related warmly to the therapist.

People coming for therapy are often stuck in a vision of themselves that is narrow and joyless. We see the therapist's job as expanding that vision and then helping clients to develop a map for getting there. Clients often need to become reacquainted with their healthy underlying strivings and to be introduced to a method for actualizing them.

The therapist's willingness to assume a healthy impulse behind the threatening behavior allowed the father to relax and feel safe enough to present other, more healthy desires. The therapist approached the father not about what he was doing wrong, but about what he *wanted*. This provided the opportunity for the therapist to help the father create a different vision of and for himself. Assuming competence often increases the possibility of building competence in this way; the process is cumulative and self-perpetuating. The desire was there, and the therapist's willingness to look for it and honor it allowed father to take pride in it. The temptation to focus on or correct the abuse would probably have been unsuccessful at that point. The therapist instead used the symptom as an entry into father's reality, and it led to his articulating a healthy desire.

3. Make a Proactive Move

Competent functioning depends on one or more people beginning to move in an effective, proactive way towards desired goals. The vision represents the awareness of what needs to change; the proactive move engages the client's commitment and courage to do so.

This may be family therapy's most important contribution to the field of psychotherapy: It is movement, not just insight, that produces change. Awareness must be paired with appropriate action. As research has established, people's belief in their efficacy is enhanced most effectively through mastery experiences. Success begets success. "Skilled efficacy builders do more than simply convey positive appraisals. In addition to cultivating people's beliefs in their capabilities, they structure situations for them in ways that bring success and avoid placing them prematurely in situations where they are likely to experience repeated failure" (Bandura, 1992, p. 327). We have found that these proactive moves are usually interpersonal in nature and are chosen with the specific goal of relationship change that directly affects the area of "pathology."

"The Epileptic Detective"   A discouraged therapist brought a difficult case to her supervisor. As part of her in-school counseling duties she was working with a very depressed, overweight girl who seemed immovable. The girl was disheartened about her entire life and future prospects, but most centrally about her epilepsy. Even with the best control medication could provide, she had one *grand mal* seizure in each of her first two years of high school (she was now a junior) and was just waiting for another. No amount of exploration of the roots of her depression and poor self-concept seemed to help.

The supervisor took a competence approach. He could not see how she could begin to feel better without enlarging her view and finding a way to see her problem differently. He suggested that the therapist turn her into a sleuth. If there were 1,500 students in her high school, and the rate of epilepsy in the general population runs between one and two per cent, how were the other 15 to 30 epileptics there managing? Were they better off than she? Did they get discouraged, too? When presented with these questions by the therapist, the girl was stunned. It had never occurred to her there was even a *single* other epileptic in her town, much less her school. She went to work on it immediately, sure that the therapist was wrong. But initial inquiries proved there were some others, though school personnel could not divulge their names. She was intrigued and began to see every student in the school as a possible fellow epileptic instead of as a "normal" snob looking down on her. She found they looked different to her.

In collaboration with the therapist, the girl decided to come out of her self-imposed isolation and see if she could flush out a few fellow sufferers. She switched her major term project in Health to epilepsy. She got an A, but no one came forward. She decided to really go for broke and made her final speech of the term in Speech and Communications on the topic, "I Am an Epileptic." The speech teacher expressed concern about the topic, but the girl was determined and defended her choice eloquently. She got an A+ for her speech. She also finally got enough visibility to draw several other students with epilepsy to her, and together they started a support group. Her depression was essentially eclipsed by this burst of focused activity, and had not recurred at one year follow-up.

4. Develop a Partnership

Competence-oriented therapy typically takes place out in the open, with the therapist developing her plan overtly and in close partnership with the family. Both the healthy striving and the unhealthy patterns are explored and understood by therapist and clients together, with the therapist serving as a guide towards healthier patterns. More often than not it is a collaboration rather than solely the therapist's clever lead. A lead is appropriate— one that expands rather than narrows the frame, that ignites the underlying hope and energy rather than maintaining the status quo. But it must then become a collaboration and a partnership.

"Push Misty for Me"   Misty, the 17-year-old identified patient, was somewhat disorganized, confused, and very anxious, but did not seem to the therapist to warrant the dire diagnosis she had received at another clinic. Her inadequacies all seemed more extreme against the backdrop of two parents and a younger sister who were very bright and articulate, if also rather rigid and joyless. The therapist felt that Misty needed a strong supportive "push" to come into her own rather than the cautious, watchful care we sometimes offer to the seemingly fragile.

After developing a good relationship with Misty in family and individual sessions, the therapist felt it was time to make a concerted push to get her going on a more mature and independent footing. She shared this map with Misty. The girl loved the idea of being more independent and "normal," but was petrified that she couldn't do it. The therapist reassured her that she would support her strongly every step of the way. Misty also cautioned the therapist that this process would make her parents awfully nervous. "They don't really trust me at all," she said. "I'm not sure they can relax and let me grow up." The therapist said she would check out the parents' readiness.

Meeting with the parents, the therapist asked their permission to pump up their daughter. "Everybody's afraid of everybody else's fragility," she said. "So you're not making use of each other. Let me push Misty to grow so she can make better use of you and what you have to offer." Misty was right: The parents had numerous anxieties about any push at all on their daughter. They were fearful that she could not handle anything but kid glove treatment. But they were willing to give it a try. "I'm going to push her to deal with you in a much more direct and mature way," the therapist cautioned, "Because she has to grow up. This is the path she needs to walk. So if you get mad at her, or she's not living up to her promises, go straight at her and I'll help her work it out with you. But if you get panicky that she's in over her head, or trying too much, bring that to me, not her. Deal with her as though she were 17. If that gets impossible, and she feels 13 to you again, deal with me directly."

In subsequent sessions, the therapist pushed Misty to work with her parents very differently and supported her changes. She reminded the girl frequently that as the oldest daughter she had the difficult job of teaching them how 17-year-olds work. Once or twice the parents asked for individual sessions (or parts of sessions) to fret about the rough edges of their daughter's growth. The therapist helped them to see it as the normal trial and error that it was, and kept them relating to her as a regular 17-year-old. At the same time, she pushed Misty to be clearer and stronger with the parents and push their limits, but also to notice that they weren't panicking or folding. Each side relied on the therapist for strength and support until they could really work the problems out directly between them. After one rather noisy disagreement about car privileges, with each side thoroughly fed up with the other, the therapist laughed appreciatively and said, "Nice fight! And no one broke! I think we're almost done."

While these cases have exemplified the importance of each of the four aspects of a competence approach, in actuality the components are not that distinct; they are interrelated and intertwined with one another in our work. What follows is an expanded case which more accurately conveys the integration of these four guidelines in theapy.

"Fathering Anew"   Greg and Linda, whose two sons were eight and six, entered therapy because of problems with eight-year-old Zack's belligerence at home and at school. There was concern about increasing estrangement in the marriage as well. The father, while a willing partner in therapy, was distracted and distant; he seemed preoccupied with work and civic affairs. The mother was more available, but felt overresponsible for everything.

Greg had been emotionally neglected by his "haughty" physician father, whom he was both in awe of and hated. Greg himself was anything but haughty. He seemed warm and empathic, sensitive to the danger of putting anyone down. He had become a very successful nurse, but he saw himself as a pale imitation of his father. In describing Zack's problems, he started in on a diatribe about his own feelings of inadequacy relative to his father. He'd had a lot of therapy and knew his pathological patterns well.

By the second session, the therapist already knew Greg's tendency to withdraw *into* his anger at his father and at one point stopped him when he did so.

Therapist: You've really worked on this hard, haven't you?
Greg: (*Nods*)
Th: And you really want to avoid having it happen again with Zack. I can see that.
Greg: (*Vigorous nod*)
Th: But it could happen again if you pay too much attention to what you needed from your dad and not enough to what Zack needs from you. He's inherited your need for really being cared about, thank God. Let me help you not get dis-

tracted by your feelings about your own dad so much that you don't tend to Zack.

Greg got this message loud and clear and felt badly about the misdirection of his focus. He started to get down on himself, and the therapist redirected him again.

Th: You've been trying to solve it with your dad for a good reason—so it won't keep on eating at you. And it's a fine focus, maybe one we'll come back to. But don't let it keep you from being with Zack now, because no one knows what he needs like you do. [This exchange constitutes the process of acknowledging healthy intentionality and accepting the pathology as an adaptive attempt gone awry.]

The therapist then began exploring with Greg why he had gone into nursing. Greg guiltily acknowledged that he had not been accepted into medical school, but added that he had not wanted to give up helping people. The therapist took in both parts but capitalized on the latter. It was helping people that fulfilled Greg. The therapist incorporated that into the budding theme.

Th: Right. That's what I thought. It's your father but with more heart. You know that nursing is medicine with warmth and love. Stop putting yourself down so much, and let's make use of what you do well.
Greg: You're right, but why doesn't it feel better to help Zack?
Th: I think it's because you leave out the heart at home, like your father did, and it hurts both you and your family. You're putting all your energy into medicine, developing your sense of adequacy there, when your son needs you terribly. Let's go to work on that first. [This exchange introduces the process of creating a different vision in therapy. The next piece translates the vision into proactive movement.]

Greg responded well. He liked the idea of focusing away from his father and onto his son. He began to connect his lack of responsiveness with his son's pattern of behavior. He started to move toward Zack emotionally and practiced not letting his own anxiety about being a good enough father get between them. Zack, of course, tested him by escalating the belligerence level, but with help Greg hung in and convinced Zack (and himself) that he was back, and there to stay. Substantial improvement resulted, as Greg brought his care and concern to bear on his son and his wife instead of lamenting his inadequacy and endlessly reworking the issues with his own father.

The therapist's first formulation in this case could easily have run to several obvious strands of psychopathology: Greg's sense of inadequacy; the possibility that he was encouraging the son's highly masculine acting out because he felt inferior for being in a "female" profession; the disowning of his own anger towards his father and investing it in his son; diverting marital tension onto the son and fighting with his wife through Zack. There are others—*and each may well be correct*. The movement in this case, however, came from the therapist's ability to see Greg's competence (caring for people) and redirect it towards his family, rather than directing Greg's attention to his pathology again. As Greg learned to invest directly and heavily in the father-son and husband-wife bonds, there was a significant change in the whole family. He stopped focusing on his *in*ability to help his son and dug in instead on his ability to be nurturant and warm. Here his partnership with the therapist facilitated his seeing his struggle differently and making changes in his interactions with his family.

Of course, a sequence like this does not produce a cure, but a beginning. It leads to new areas of problems and difficulties, not to a smooth linear progression towards improvement. This father ran into multiple internal concerns (e.g., feelings of inadequacy) and systemic concerns (e.g., Zack's bond with the mother) that needed attention. But the underlying dynamic of the therapy remained the same. It had moved from his own pathological construction of "I'm less than my father as a professional and his sorry equal as a father" to "I can care for people openly and lovingly (maybe even more than my father could), and I want to start with my own family." In the process he also came to see his father as frustrated and sad about his inability to be a better father. He started to feel that his father would have been proud of his ability to both nurture patients and love his family directly and effectively.

There are a number of interesting competence issues in this case. For example, there was the three-generational recursive pattern of estrangement between father and son and overinvolvement between mother and son. In other therapeutic approaches, this might be the focus. In a competence model, however, the first focus is on supporting and developing the father-son relationship in the best way we can. A *primary* goal in therapy is building a structure that works, not necessarily "resolving" what doesn't work.

At the same time, we think it is imperative to have a healthy respect for what does not work. In part, Greg's struggles with his son came from precise patterns learned from interactions with his father. Greg had put a great deal of time into identifying these, and they were important to him. To feel helped by the therapist, not merely redirected, Greg needed to know that these past struggles were understood and acknowledged. Through the process of understanding Greg's patterns with his father and his son, the therapist could identify the underlying healthy striving within them—in this case, Greg's strong wish to master the father-son relationship. Together, the therapist and Greg could then create a different, more adaptive path for achieving these goals.

Others before us have certainly identified the importance of helping a client develop a vision for where they want to go as a component of creating change. The "Miracle Question" developed by de Shazer (1985), for example, does just this. Specifically, it asks the client to identify how he would be behaving if the problem had, by some miracle, resolved itself. Through the process of getting what de Shazer calls a "thick description" of these changes, the therapist is helping the client to develop a clearer vision of where he wants to be and how he would behave differently. The solution-oriented therapists do a good job of developing both a vision with the client and a path for getting there. (In this case, the vision might have been Zack behaving and Greg interacting with him more nurturantly and enjoyably.)

What they do not do, however, is to actively disconnect the energy entangled in the pathological struggle and reconnect it to the healthy strivings. We think a key aspect of the success of this case was Greg becoming aware of the healthy urge in both his struggle with his father and his pursuit of nursing. He was then encouraged to convert that same energy into establishing a closer relationship with his son. Developing his competence made use of his past struggles rather than ignoring them.

It is certainly possible to accuse us of skimming over the problem and merely reframing a mess as adequate. We never intend to do that, and hold no brief for it as a method. In this case, for example, the move was not one of avoiding the problem, but of attending to a different part of the pattern. Greg was obsessed with his father and, therefore, was ignoring his son, though he had developed precisely the abilities Zack needed. Rather than attend to the failure with his father, we attended to his success as a nurse and the potential for making use of his carefully developed sensitivity to help his son. He is more apt to change his behavior towards his son by using a competence he has already developed but not identified, than by reviewing his difficulties with his own father. Skimming over the problem would avoid or ignore the issues with his own father and focus on doing better with his son. ("I don't know about your dad, but I'm sure you really care about your son!") Again, we want to use the energy he directs toward the battle with his own father and redirect it toward the issues with Zack. ("You've developed in yourself the warmth you needed to get from your dad, but you're wasting it. Don't overlook your son by focusing on your dad.") In this way, we often actively redirect energy stuck in unhealthy struggles back to a healthy path. All energy has some healthy motive, and we try to find and harness that motive.

The pathology focus will often convince therapists of the immutability of patterns — the longer you gaze on the pathological roots, the more tangled and deeply set they seem. A therapist can quickly blunt his own hopeful edge with too much creative thinking about what cannot possibly happen. On the other hand, a pure solution focus can make therapists cavalier about a client's struggles. Such a focus orients the client toward his desired outcomes, but does not take into account the sense of loss the client may feel as he begins to change his patterns.

Part of our job as therapists is to provide hope and possibility as well as insight and working through. For that we always want to test the potential for forward movement as well as the need for retrospective investigation and resolution. In this case, as is often true, they complemented each other. The proactive moves by Greg toward Zack brought to light anxieties, but motivated change. The retrospective work was different than it had been before because of Greg's new experience with his son. As he became able to see his and Zack's difficulties with each other as understandable, normal ones, he softened his angry view of his father and their difficulties. As he became less critical of his father, he also lightened up on himself. It is a circle that proceeds *mutatis mutandis*, not a linear process. But the proactive step—the working with strength and positive energy—is a crucial part of the circle.

Investigating Strengths

The process of developing a vision with clients, mentioned earlier, is an important one. Therapists are usually trained to see what people cannot do: where their pathology inhibits, or might inhibit, their healthy functioning. We have *no* training, as a rule, in seeing the reverse: what people can do or have done, how they may manage. Similarly, we do not know how to investigate or articulate how their healthy functioning may inhibit their psychopathology. For example, Greg had devoted his life to developing a warm, nurturant bearing that was different from his father's hard, surgical one. It was partly compensatory, built on going into nursing rather than medicine, but it was also a very adaptive use of his desire to be different from his father. Seeing that strength in Greg, understanding its importance in the family, and bringing it out as an active element in the treatment are all crucial skills—and desperately underdeveloped among many therapists.

It is also interesting in this case that the therapist reached to a strength that was closely tied to a weakness and used both parts. In appealing to Greg's sense of being better at nurturing people than his father was, the therapist actually made *use* of the unconscious competition in a way some people might disapprove of, especially if they view Greg's feeling toward his father as purely "oedipal psychopathology." There is also a clearly healthy element to Greg's pattern. He developed the strengths his father lacked, a lack that hurt him. If one focuses on the unhealthy side of Greg's behavior, it becomes something angry, needing resolution. If, on the other hand, one looks at its healthy side—making up a lack within the family by developing needed compassion—it becomes energy with obvious and important potential. If you see it as a strength, Greg already has what Zack needs and has only to use it. If you see it as a weakness, Greg is far from being able to nurture his son because he was not nurtured and is still angry. Most of his previous therapy had emphasized his anger toward his father exclusively. That leaves lots of work to do to redress Greg's problem before he can even begin to focus on helping Zack.

In a deficit model, only the inadequacy is of real interest. In a competence paradigm, the therapist is responsible for seeking out both weakness and strength, and for seeing how they fit together. The diagnostician of pathology looks at the symptoms and patterns for the damage they have done and what other pathology they indicate. This tends toward a very one-sided view that credits the person little or not at all with broader motives or healthy aspirations.

"Norman's Complaints"   A depressed family came to therapy with a push from their new social worker. There were three children—Danny (17), Monica (14), and Norman (11), but only Norman came because the parents could not find the other two when it was time to come. It had been an awful four weeks for the family, starting with father losing his job and ending with their being evicted from their apartment for non-payment of rent. They had just found a new place, and no one liked it. The children had been railing against the parents since they moved in, with Norman leading the attack.

Norman was foul-mouthed and hostile in the session as well. The parents attacked back by pointing out his inadequacies and shortfalls. Within ten minutes, multiple pathologies were obvious. They were all depressed, hostile, and hurt. The son seemed to be antisocial and incorrigible; the parents seemed immature and disorganized. When the parents got crosswise of each other, the marriage looked hopeless. Father had lost several jobs previously: depression? alcohol? drugs? The mother seemed bright but flaky, an unlikely ally in reversing the family's downward spiral. The therapist looked ready to give up. He appeared overwhelmed by the family's crisis and their limited resources. He began to track symptoms exclusively; not surprisingly, the family began to look even worse.

At this point, a competence-minded supervisor behind the one-way mirror called in: "Why are they here? Lots of people get pushed toward counseling by worried social workers, but few come — especially given all their recent crises. Find out why they came and for what they're hoping. I think these people have a vision of something better, and the situation hurts them all so badly precisely because it is so far from where they want to be. Get to know their vision so that you see them more fully."

As the therapist embarked on this more hopeful journey, a palpable shift occurred. Father, mother, and Norman all contributed stories of better times and even laughed together a bit. The therapist tracked the contrasts between their past and current situations. In particular, this helped the parents to identify and empathize with Norman's painful losses (friends, home, dignity, and a neighborhood family that liked him). They understood what he was coping with, as they were struggling with the same losses.

But the current losses and failure remained the therapist's prime concern. He was more positively engaged with the family, but still could not see how he might make use of "the good old days." Again, the supervisor suggested a more positive focus, this time encouraging the therapist to look for Norman's underlying striving. Perhaps his behavior was both a protest against failure and a real change, not his inherent personality. If so, the therapist was encouraged to help the parents understand it as such and get him to redirect that energy in a way that was more adaptive for him. Norman was right to protest, but he needed to do so in a way that wasn't unproductive and hurtful for everyone else.

When the therapist returned to the room, all three family members agreed that Norman's behavior was primarily a change from his earlier good behavior. The parents were encouraged to find out what hurt him so badly that he was suddenly being so nasty, and to try to understand it. They did this fairly well, and Norman, feeling heard, calmed down considerably. But he retained three strong complaints: He hated feeling poor, he never got to see his old friends, and he had no freedom. The parents responded reasonably to the complaints, since they were feeling more in control and less defensive. They agreed that they also hated feeling poor and were struggling against it. They told him what steps they had taken to make things better, and he was pleased. They also worked out a "deal" with him, whereby they would try to address his complaints, but he had to lower the pitch of his attacks. The father, far from being stuck in the failure role, took the lead in requesting Norman's help in turning the family's fortunes around. Norman responded with a sarcastic comment that barely hid his obvious pleasure in being asked to contribute: "Don't worry, you guys. I'll rob a bank and give it all to you!" To which the therapist replied, "Are you nuts?! Keep some for yourself!" They left with a promise to help each other through the crisis, and Norman started talking about getting a work permit so he could help out.

With disaster averted, the case felt infinitely better to the therapist. But the disaster was largely iatrogenic. The family entered in disarray and hostility, but the therapist doused their fire with gasoline as he trapped himself in a hopeless tracking of their multiple symptoms. When he approached them with an attitude that re-embedded them in aspects of themselves they felt good about and could build from, they looked and acted entirely differently. Symptoms and problems are real, but no more real than strengths and resources.

What if, when the therapist explored the family's pre-crisis state, he had only found prior crises and disasters? Imagine a tale of alcoholic functioning, lost jobs, marital misery, borderline functioning. What then? The first response is that it would change the process significantly. We would not try to make the above scenario work out of the strength of *our* vision; we would continue to look for the workable strengths in the family's vision.

Looking past the obvious weakness to the hidden strengths, and flushing them out for active use, is a skill most therapists need to develop. In general, we were all taught the opposite, that the genius of the therapist is in looking past apparent strengths to hidden weaknesses. But the fundamental skills of seeing, respecting, and making use of people's strengths, resources, even their genius, is grossly neglected in training and supervision. In these cases, it came (as it often does) as a pleasant surprise to the families. But for this focus to work it must be real. If the therapist invents a strength he *wishes* the person had, and credits it to him for strategic purposes, it is an empty vessel. Part of the value of the observation of competence is that you are touching something real and vital in the person's makeup, as well as something often neglected. Sometimes you have to reach fairly far to find it.

"The Novice Feminist"   Tammy was a 16-year-old whose family had recently moved to our city. Her father had requested a company transfer away from a larger city because Tammy had fallen in love with Tony, a ne'er-do-well 19-year-old local surfer. Tammy's parents saw Tony as a hustling, irresponsible bum who would waste their daughter's potential. Tammy saw him as a demigod, even though he had already slapped her around a couple of times and gotten her pregnant. (When she called to tell him she was pregnant, he responded that it could be anybody's child, and hung up.) He had always treated her badly, but it just made her more devoted. The parents had told her over and over that she was too good for him, but to no avail. They finally reluctantly and angrily moved away to try to break Tony's spell. Of course, it only got stronger. Now they wanted therapy to fix her so that Tony would really be out of her life for good, and she would not care about him anymore.

Not surprisingly, Tammy aggressively held her position in therapy. They didn't understand Tony. They didn't see what a catch he was. She would never love anyone else. The therapist saw Tammy alone to see if he could find a way out of this impasse. Having three daughters around her age, he worried about her position: She was denying all the facts of the relationship and was clinging to a dangerous fantasy. Here was a young girl setting herself up for abuse and abandonment but blind to it. She was using her ferocity *against* her parents rather than *for* herself. The therapist decided to see if that could be rechanneled.

Therapist: So you think you're *not* too good for him.
Tammy: Absolutely not.
Th: If you were, what would you do?
Tammy: But I'm not!
Th: I know. But if by some fluke you were, what would you do? Just imagine.

Tammy: I'd get rid of him right away.

Th: I'll bet. You have a lot of pride?

Tammy: Sure I do! And everyone envied me being with Tony. Anyone would tell you I was the lucky one, not him!

Th: So if you thought you were too good for him you'd dump him? (*Tammy nods*) How would you know? How does a woman know if she's too good for a guy? (*This stumps her momentarily, but she recovers.*)

Tammy: Well, like, if he's not nice to her. If he drops her for other girls or two-times her or just—you know—isn't reliable. Isn't nice.

Th: Yeah, that makes sense. [*No, it doesn't!* Tony is reported to have done *all* of those things and more. But, if I jump in with logic I'll lose her. She likes the idea that she is too proud to go with a loser, even if her parents and I think she's doing it. So I play dumb.] So you'd *never* go with a guy who would do you like that?

Tammy: No way. Never.

Th: So if you went down there to visit, how would you want Tony to treat you?

Tammy: I'd expect him to treat me like a queen—take me nice places, stay away from other girls, pick me up on time, stuff like that.

Th: He should really treat you right. Then you'd know you weren't too good for him?

Tammy: Right.

Th: So how could we find out if he's good enough for you? If he knows how to treat a woman right?

Tammy quickly suggested a weekend visit with Tony. To her surprise, the therapist agreed, but began to turn it into an anthropological field trip for her to find out if Tony was too good for her or vice versa. Tammy just wanted to rush off and try it, but the therapist insisted they spend several weeks delineating what would be "good enough" behavior on Tony's part. In so doing, they discussed what a woman should expect and drew up a list of particulars. (Of course, she never accused Tony of anything; it was always in the abstract.) The longer they worked on it, the more she focused on her right to certain kinds of treatment: A boyfriend should exhibit respectful interest in what she wanted to do; he should be attentive and not just try to get her into bed immediately. She began to sound like a novice feminist. She didn't love Tony less, but she began to be more thoughtful about herself.

Finally, she and the therapist approached her parents together, and she asked permission to go back to their old city, stay with a girlfriend, and see Tony. The parents objected at first, but with persuasion and explanation from the therapist, they finally allowed it. Tammy set out to determine if she was too good for Tony, fairly sure that she was not. But, for the first time, she was clear about the criteria.

The upshot was that Tony treated her fairly well, with the exception of an insensitive overeagerness to bed her that made her mad. But, less blinded by the battle with her parents, Tammy found him boring and shallow. She wanted to continue to be his girl, but from a distance.

The crux of this case was not whether Tammy was freed from Tony's spell, but how to teach her about her underlying competence. From that she learned how to ask the right questions and approach the relationship differently. Instead of fighting her parents automatically and using her sense of entitlement to feel, "I must have what I want," she went off to challenge Tony and to see if she got decent treatment. Her sense of entitlement now became her strength rather than her weakness. The healthy part of it was revived. It changed how she saw Tony; more importantly, it changed how she saw herself. And it certainly changed how she worked in therapy. Before this focus evolved, she saw the therapist as merely another nosy adult. When they focused on what she deserved as a woman, she became interested and energized.

As in the previous case, Tammy benefitted from an altered sense of what is "healthy." Her strength was her desire to be well treated and feel special. Her weakness was her sense of entitlement, and needing to have what she wanted regardless of its appropriateness. The latter blinded her to Tony's faults. The therapy rechanneled the energy that had been stuck in battling her parents, into the healthy direction of figuring out what she deserved in a relationship and insisting on it. This resulted in Tammy feeling more competent and effective.

Development of a Project

We have introduced a number of elements that we consider important to the progress of therapy: competence, courage, vision, and partnership. These could easily overwhelm the therapist if she tried to account for each separately, and track each one's progress. What is needed is a central event in therapy, which pulls these elements together and imposes some order and meaning on them. That is partly the function of the vision or theme, as discussed earlier in this chapter. But themes need to be made concrete to some extent, or they get lost.

We find that in our work there frequently evolves a central issue, which pulls these many parts together. Sometimes it is entirely straightforward and functional, sometimes it is powerfully metaphorical. We have come to call this issue "the project": a task or series of tasks that organizes and underlines the family's energy for and movement toward fulfilling their healthy striving.

When Greg's energy was redirected toward his son and the development of his competence as a father, and away from his own father and his feelings of failure, a natural project evolved. Greg began to focus on how to nurture his son in the way he had always longed to be nurtured. When the therapist led Tammy toward an evolution of her consciousness of what a woman should expect, then a project slowly took shape for her as well.

Projects pull apparently disparate issues together via the mechanism of a central action focus. They also serve as a platform on which the budding sense of efficacy may be developed. They give the therapist and client a structure that they can then work on together, and a direction in which to move. A good project actualizes the vision and organizes the partnership. Rather than the therapist being in the one-up position of teaching, correcting, and critiquing, he can serve as a partner in bringing about something whose value he and the client share.

For example, the project that evolved with Tammy led to a different kind of partnership with the therapist. Instead of critiquing and containing her, he helped her to develop a more powerful sense of herself as a woman. Instead of convincing her of her worth, the project provided her a platform for developing her *own* view of it. She designed the test and became the tester.

A project is not a *sine qua non* of good therapy. We do not set out to create a project; we try to create an atmosphere and a partnership in which the project can evolve. It often does, but not in every case. For example, in the case of Norman, a project did not evolve in the first session. The work was on track and appropriate, but there was no need yet for a central structure; it would have been premature and forced. We do not advocate developing projects in therapy for projects' sake. A forced and contrived project is worse then no project at all. The therapist needs to be patient and watchful for the emergence of an action-oriented focus, but not demanding. Developing a project with a family is a natural consequence of encouraging them to act on their underlying competence in a way that reorients them to where they want to go.

A competence focus is a way of organizing therapy to deal actively with what is dysfunctional, and proactively with where people need to be heading to return to better functioning. The therapist who works in this way needs to make himself responsible for finding and holding a center in therapy. The content of the center must come from the family; establishing and maintaining it, or adjusting it when it is off, is the therapist's task. Usually, the most crucial aspect of that task is moving from the client's problem to the part of the client that offers a way out: the resources or strength or genius that can be harnessed in order to escape the psychological thicket.

four

HEALTHY INTENTIONS, UNHEALTHY OUTCOMES

Pathology is not a problem to be cured, but the soul's way of working on itself.

— *James Hillman*

The Deficit Model

Psychopathology is an elusive concept. Unlike physiopathology, it is almost entirely theoretically derived. What is viewed as pathological in the psychological realm varies dramatically depending upon the theoretical lens one uses. The variations are not only large but often irreconcilable. And how any theory construes psychopathology will determine how its followers try to repair or restore functioning.

The historical accident that made Freud a physician who thought in medical metaphors has cast a long shadow. He tried to fit the discoveries that he was making about people's emotional makeup into the mechanistic medical model in which he had been trained. Since physical pathology always had substratas of dysfunctional organs or cells, he made the same assumption about psychopathology. Each layer of emotional sickness was thought to rest on a deeper layer, and the investigation of these deeper layers was thought to be appropriate treatment. The deeper one went, the better; the more attention one paid to the psychopathology, the closer one was to the deepest layer of disease, and the greater the chance for a cure.

This construction of what goes wrong in human functioning has persisted for a long time. For many years after Freud's original formulations, and up until quite recently, people have built on the illness model. Maladaptive behavior is routinely thought of as illness or deficit, the product of a fundamental sickness within the person. As a result, we have become almost completely deficit-oriented (Cowen, 1991; Garmezy, 1987). Many models of diagnosis and treatment offer complete schemes for investigating what is wrong with the person, but virtually none for what is functional or effective. We are likely to study people's difficulties *ad absurdum*, but altogether ignore their assets. As Garmezy (1987) points out, "Health, not illness, is the norm of the society; resistance, not capitulation to mental disorders is the norm; adaptation and recovery from stress, and not breakdown, is the way of the majority" (p 164). An exclusive focus on psychopathology, from frank illness to the "psychopathology of everyday life," leaves us oblivious to patterns of health and striving for health.

Problems of a Deficit Model

One ramification of the old perspective is that our fixation on deficits and pathology becomes a circular process. When we look for pathology, we usually find it; we conclude that it is the "true" representation of the person rather than the product of our lens. What we believe is insightful understanding of a client may in fact be a function of our particular perspective. It can become a closed system: We build upon the existence of pathology, thereby exaggerating its significance. Garmezy (1987) notes that " . . . the exclusive focus of the mental health disciplines on pathogenic processes can best be explained by philosopher Abraham Kaplan's 'law of the hammer.' Simply put, the law's basic postulate is: 'Give a child a hammer and everything the kid sees will need pounding'" (p. 164). We are trained to see deficits, weaknesses, and symptoms, *and to derive our role from their presence*. And so we see them, often to the exclusion of other observations.

Another result of a psychopathology orientation is that we tend to confuse the patterns of dysfunction with the person. What begins as a descriptor of certain characteristics associated with a particular problem becomes a descriptor of the entire person. We may become so fixated on dysfunction that we lose contextual awareness and begin to see pathology as the totality of people, or at least as their most important quality. "She *is* an hysteric," we say, in a classic confusion of part with whole, or "He *is* an obsessive compulsive." We confuse people's dysfunction with their basic selves. Certainly we all have deficits, but none of us assumes that those deficits are our primary, much less our total, identity. While we may accept that, at times, we are selfish, flirtatious, or finicky, most of us would resist being entirely subsumed under the label narcissistic, hysteric, or obsessive-compulsive. Yet, we tend to do it to our clients routinely. We are all familiar with examples of everyday behavior that can be seen very differently depending on the orientation of the observer. For example, a woman addresses her husband in a shrill, caustic tone and uses demeaning words to describe him. She can be called anything from a "castrating bitch" to an abused wife who is fighting back. A more intrapsychic formulation will focus on her rage and her internal functioning. A more systemic formulation will look at the interaction between the two people, and the interpersonal pattern that foments this kind of communication. The lens adopted dictates whether one sees adaptation or pathology in every behavior. Too often our models are biased towards deficits.

The deficit model also orients us to look at psychopathological events as fixed, rather than as a process. The psychopathology focus becomes a way of trying to pin down the personality, but with a sole emphasis on naming certain symptoms or tendencies, and then reifying them. These reified entities are then seen as inherent and fundamental, instead of as part of the kaleidoscopic tumble through which people evolve. Somehow we have come to assume that these pathological parts of people are more basic and real than their strengths.

Finally, a psychopathology focus does not suggest a way out of the pathological pattern. The traditional theories of psychopathology direct us to the type and the magnitude of the deficit, but offer few clues for attending to and working with the frustrated desires that underlie the dysfunction. The assumption is that once the internal conflict is understood, behavioral change is the natural consequence, but this has not always been borne out. Focusing primarily on dysfunction does not provide us with a map for moving toward new behaviors. We are more skilled at teaching people how to investigate their flaws than we are at teaching them effective ways to change them.

Incremental vs. Entity Theories

Change and development are the business of life. We are all constantly growing and changing. This is most obvious with children. As Combrinck-Graham persuasively argues (1989), a deficit approach is particularly unhelpful in working with children because of their inherent plasticity. Change is their natural, virtually constant state. They continually adapt, adjust, and take advantage of new possibilities. Mastery is a constant, incremental flow that runs through their lives. While this process is most apparent with children, it is no less true for adults.

A psychopathology focus tends to move us away from a respectful awareness of the constancy of change and toward an inaccurate sense of people as fixed entities, permanently endowed with certain psychopathological traits. This fixed, immutable quality of the psychopathology orientation is one we find particularly erroneous and unhelpful. People's lives are an ongoing process, with both functional and dysfunctional patterns that are clearly apparent, but not fixed.

Social psychologists have wrestled with the fixed entity vs. incremental process view of various abilities in ways that illuminate this issue. Dweck (1986), for example, found that some parents socialize their children to believe in either an "entity" or an "incremental" idea of their intellectual abilities. An entity view holds that intelligence is fixed; one has a set amount, and it won't change. Whether the message is "You're really smart" or "You're not very smart," the metamessage is "It's done. You've got what you've got, and now you just work with it." An incremental view holds that intelligence is an evolving, changing ability that is affected by hard work, concentration, etc. The metamessage here is, "It's up to you how smart you are. You're in charge of it."

Which theory one subscribes to can have significant implications for how obstacles are dealt with, and for the response to success or failure. For example, researchers have found that girls are more likely to endorse a fixed entity theory of their intelligence (Leggett, 1985), and so show decreased performance following an initial failure (Licht & Dweck, 1984). As Markus et al. (1990) conclude, "Improvement and fundamental self-change are more possible for people with an incremental theory of their abilities" (p. 216). When faced with a failure, they are more able to see it as a setback rather than as proof of their inherent inadequacy.

We hold the same position relative to psychopathology. If either client or therapist holds a fundamental "fixed entity" theory of the client's psychopathology, change becomes much more difficult. If dysfunction can be seen as an active process ("I get anxious in certain situations if I'm not prepared for them.") instead of as a fixed entity ("I have an anxiety disorder" or "I am a panic attack case."), there is much more hope and possibility in working with it. A sense of problems as changeable is very important for people's sense of hope for improvement. Seligman's term, "learned helplessness" (1975), comes precisely from the observation that if people see their dilemma as permanent and fixed, they will not act to change it. If we see psychopathology as fixed and permanent, we will hinder rather than facilitate our clients' ability to change.

Other people have worked on this same notion. For example, Michael White and David Epston (1990), in Australia and New Zealand respectively, have developed a wonderfully incremental way of looking at dysfunction that emphasizes its susceptibility to being changed. After clarifying what the problem is and how much harm it has done, they work to help a client become aware of how much he knows and does *already*, not just potentially, that enhances his functioning and leads to a better outcome. They then work to build his awareness of how much control he has, and help him to practice it in a variety of ways. In a very direct fashion, they enhance his sense of control over his own outcomes without in the least ignoring or minimizing the dysfunctional patterns. It is a highly effective move away from the idea of psychopathology as a fixed entity.

Health Orientations

If we are not focusing on psychopathology in therapy, then what *should* we focus on? There have been several movements in the field of mental health that emphasize people's health above their deficits. The humanistic position of Carl Rogers (1961), for example, assumed that people are naturally good, healthy, and worthy. He challenged the view that people have inherent psychopathologies. Rather, he viewed psychopathology as the result of people adopting external conditions to their sense of worth. The therapy that follows from this theory provides the client with "unconditional positive regard" in a nonjudgmental relationship in which the client's self-actualizing abilities will flourish. It is an approach designed to let the normal health shine through.

Other theorists have also concentrated primarily on health. For example, Milton Erickson (Haley, 1973) was much less interested in the roots or causes of people's problems than in techniques that would move them toward solutions. He viewed people as possessing the resources, within themselves or their systems, to make the changes that they needed to make. He felt therapy " . . . was predicated upon the assumption that there is a strong normal tendency for the personality to adjust if given the opportunity" (O'Hanlon & Weiner-Davis, 1989, p. 16, quoting Rossi).

The field of family therapy has long led the way in the search for a health vs. a deficit orientation. As Minuchin and Fishman (1981, p. 268) noted early on: "Family therapists are finding that an exploration of strengths is essential to challenge family dysfunctions." Satir (1988) focused on growth and finding alternative paths, Boszormenyi-Nagy (1987) emphasized positive connotation, Madanes (1984) searched for a family's underlying benevolence, and Minuchin (1974), himself, believed in the inherent strengths and resources of a family.

The solution-oriented theorists (de Shazer, 1988, 1991; O'Hanlon & Weiner-Davis, 1989) build on this foundation as well, focusing their "search for solutions" on a presumption of a natural desire to do better. They have been highly creative in finding ways to direct people towards their strengths and are much more interested in those than in pathology. For the most part, they reject psychopathology as a useful concept. de Shazer (1991), for example, suggests that "specific causes" for problems cannot be known; the concept of psychopathology must be set aside in favor of an orientation towards solutions co-created between family and therapist. This model "normalizes" behavior. As O'Hanlon and Weiner-Davis note, solution-oriented therapists tend to view problems or symptoms " . . . not as pathological manifestations but as ordinary difficulties of life" (1989, p. 93). This emphasis actively moves away from the problem and toward a solution. The solution-oriented therapists are interested in developing and expanding a person's solutions, not investigating his problems.

Critics of the solution-oriented approach (Nichols & Schwartz, 1991; Wylie, 1990) point out that with a sole focus on solutions and problem resolution, the therapist may be induced to minimize, deny, or overlook problems that need to be taken seriously. In contrast to the deficit model, which tends to underestimate health, this approach may miss important and/or useful aspects of dysfunction. Whereas the psychodynamic approach can have tunnel vision for problems, the solution-oriented approach can have it for solutions—a different hammer, but a hammer nonetheless.

Rather than viewing behavior as either healthy or pathological, we can be more helpful to clients if we are respectful of all components of their behavior. If we try to recognize and learn from their limitations and their assets, we will be better able to help them bring their full resources to bear on effecting the kinds of changes they desire.

How then can we be respectful of and make use of psychopathology, but not become mired in it? In the same vein, how do we notice and promote strengths and health without overdoing it and becoming obliviously optimistic and disingenuous? Are there models for striking a balance, for making use of both sets of information? We believe so.

A Holistic Theory

That humans are multidimensional rather than unidimensional has long been a cornerstone of personality theories. However, very few theorists have developed multidimensional conceptualizations of people that attend equally to their pathology and their health. We have found the theory of Andras Angyal (1965) helpful in this regard. Angyal developed a holistic theory of personality and problem formation, which postulates that in each of us there are two competing systems — one "healthy" and the other "neurotic" — battling for dominance.

Each system organizes the world differently. When operating within their healthy system, people view themselves and others with "loving confidence." They are aware of their strengths, empowered by their capabilities, and comfortable about their limitations. When the neurotic system is dominant, however, they approach the world with a "fearful diffidence." They tend to view people and situations as potentially hostile and cold. They are focused only on their own and their world's limitations and retreat into a defensive, almost paranoid stance when engaging with others. (It is interesting to compare this view to Scheinfeld's research cited in Chapter 2. The language and concepts are similar, though the theoretical backgrounds differ markedly.)

Angyal suggests that both systems are fully operational in all of us and that we constantly shift back and forth between the two. A person differs from day to day, and even moment to moment, in her own healthy-neurotic balance. We differ from each other in the ease or difficulty we have staying in the healthy system. Following is an example of how these systems interact.

Susan, a 20-year-old mother of a colicky newborn, struggles all day to meet her baby's demands. Despite his incessant crying, she continues to approach him soothingly. She tries everything she knows to appease him, is pleased when he quiets for a bit and accepts it as a new challenge when he begins to cry again. Even with significant provocation, she manages to continue to approach her child with "loving confidence." She operates out of her healthy system. Then Sam, her husband, comes home. Having had a hard day himself, he is somewhat preoccupied and gives her a distracted "hello" as he heads for the telephone to make a business call. In the midst of this, the baby begins to cry, and Susan explodes. She accuses Sam of being cold and uncaring, of expecting her to do everything for the baby, and, further, of acting as if his life and interests are more important than her. She slams out of the house and doesn't return for two hours.

Angyal would say that Susan is now operating out of her "neurotic system," a system that, at the moment, seems logical and coherent to Susan but that, in fact, minimizes her ability to connect with and master her world. While the content of Susan's attack is most likely accurate, the way she shares it does not really get her what she wants—increased connection with and respect from Sam. Once tapped, her reservoir of past feelings of being unloved and unlovable move her to approach Sam with "fearful diffidence." Neither system by itself *is* Susan. Both systems are equally a part of her. She moves between the two depending upon internal and external demands and resources; the baby and her husband rouse the two differently.

Two Interconnected Systems

Angyal emphasizes that these two diametrically opposed ways of being are not isolated thoughts, feelings, or behaviors, but are organized systems. Each organizes differently our basic needs for mastery and belonging. What results is a "dual patterning of personality." For Susan, the healthy system is fueled by her successes at mastery and belonging with the baby. Her neurotic system is triggered when she feels ignored by her husband and becomes overwhelmed by feelings of isolation or inadequacy. Instead of making direct efforts at mastering the situation (asking Sam to be more attentive), she puts much of her effort into protecting herself. Her protective attack, meant to provide a safe retreat from the perceived dangers of the world, actually furthers her sense of isolation and exacerbates her feelings of disappointment and hurt. She is in a cycle of seeing fewer opportunities for love and mastery, and thus of experiencing more isolation and inadequacy. Angyal points out that anxiety, thought by many to be the basis of psychopathology, comes from the German word for "narrow." When people operate in their "neurotic system," they are "narrowed in"; they see fewer possibilities for success and connectedness. When the healthy system dominates, people operate with an expansive view. Success begets success.

According to Angyal, the fact that there are two diametrically opposed systems in each of us explains why, when taken out of context, it is easy to see very different meanings in most behaviors. Each behavior *potentially* serves both the healthy and unhealthy systems. The power of reframing, then, becomes clear; all behavior has a connection to both our healthy and unhealthy systems. Empathy can mask dependency, love can mask possessiveness, anger can mask concern, and vice versa. Both feelings in each pair are "real." Angyal also points out that the two systems are intertwined; they are formed in relation to one another, not in isolation. Our psychopathology coevolves with our health. When a person seeks mastery or belonging, successes form the nucleus of the healthy system and failures form the nucleus of the unhealthy system. (And most situations have aspects of both success and failure.) According to Angyal, this interconnectedness between the healthy and the neurotic systems explains why people are resistant to the therapist's attempts to "cut out" their pathology. As he notes, the positive component of resistance is loyalty—loyalty to old patterns that have been there for a long time. Despite the pain and distortions caused by the psychopathology, giving it up can feel like a threat to one's integrity.

The interconnectedness between the two systems also means that the motivational energy that feeds pathological behavior can readily be transferred to healthy behavior when the connection is made. Angyal states that "Health is present potentially in its full power in the most destructive, most baneful, most shameful behavior" (1965, p. 104). Thus, motivational force has to be redirected back to the healthy system.

If one assumes a basic competence in people, an underlying striving for mastery and belonging, then symptoms can more readily be seen as adaptive attempts gone awry. The focus turns away from a person's failed pattern and toward his powerful need. If we see symptoms this way, we see them with much more hope and possibility. They become the basis for movement toward something better, a form of *potential energy*, rather than a disease that, at best, must be neutralized.

"Playing Ball on the Same Team"   The Smith family sought family therapy at the suggestion of the Juvenile Court intake officer. Mr. Smith had requested that the court "scare" his 15-year-old son into behaving (which he defined as going to school, giving up drugs, respecting his father) before it was too late. The son, Junior, would turn 16 in five months, and Mr. Smith viewed that

as the beginning of manhood and, thus, the end of his ability to influence his son. In the first family session, it quickly became apparent that the battle between father and son was mutual. Mr. Smith was cold, critical, and unrelenting in his efforts to "teach" Junior how he should behave. Similarly, Junior only knew how to activate his father's sense of inadequacy and irritation. Furious about his father's past treatment of his mother (affairs, drinking, abuse) and of him, Junior's efforts at respectful dialogue with his father were minimal.

However, this classic father-son struggle also had roots in the "health system" of both. There were competent components to their battling that needed underlining and expanding. For example, Mr. Smith's disappointment at his son's involvement in drugs was largely fueled by a special love he had for his firstborn and high hopes that his namesake avoid the same pitfalls that had limited him. He wanted his son to master what he had failed. The healthy component for Junior was that he felt lucky that, unlike most of his friends, he at least had a father. Having a man in his life who was involved (albeit critically) and who insisted that Junior could do better than he was doing clearly mattered to him. Yet they were both stuck in approaching each other with "fearful diffidence." They each had easy access to a view of themselves as unlovable and the other as hostile; they had limited access to healthier views of each other.

But the health was there. The same energy used in their battling was also fueled by an underlying desire to feel respected by and connected with each other. Therapy began focusing on how they could learn to become men *together*, rather than at the expense of the other. With this perspective, the therapist went "health hunting." Mr. Smith was invited to tell the therapist (with Junior listening) why the job of fathering was so important to him. He revealed that more than anything else he wanted to be the kind of father that he had never had. His father had abandoned the family when he was five, and he had sworn to himself that he would never abandon his son. In fact, his life was organized around fathering. He had married his wife because she was pregnant and had stayed in an unsatisfying marriage because of the children. He saw fighting with Junior as a sacrifice he had to make, because he knew of no other way to fight *for* him. Mr. Smith softened as he told his story. Because he felt his intentions had been acknowledged, he was then able to agree that his approach with Junior was not working: He just did not know what else to do.

Junior also softened somewhat as he listened to how central fathering was to his Dad and how hard he had tried, albeit unsuccessfully. Since teaching was synonymous with mastering fatherhood for Mr. Smith, the therapist invited Junior to think about what, if anything, he might want his father to teach him. After initial strutting about already being a man and not needing anything, he mentioned basketball. His father, it turned out, was a basketball legend in their community and had been considered college material until he had dropped out of school to marry and support his pregnant girlfriend (Junior's mother). He had stopped taking his son to play basketball with him two years ago because of the deterioration of their relationship; for the same reason, Junior had stopped asking to go. They were encouraged to start again, but with a new focus. Rather than trying to beat one another, Mr. Smith was asked to teach his son what he knew about basketball while playing on the same team. They were reminded that they had plenty of "dirt" on each other, but what they needed was a respectful partnership with one another. The same energy that had been used previously to catch the other in errors was now to be directed toward helping the other so that they could beat the opposing team.

Redirecting Energy

As we have noted, we view dysfunction as the result of attempted solutions gone awry. Mr. Smith's critical, "uncaring" stance with Junior was very much a product of his strong caring about his son and fears about not being able to father him successfully. By viewing his efforts as misdirected energy rather than solely as psychopathology, the therapist was able to redirect part of the energy into more "healthful" behaviors. Like Angyal, we believe in what he called the "primacy of health." And, like him, we see the goal of therapy as restoring the healthy system to dominance.

Reorienting Mr. Smith and his son toward the solution of working together on a mutually rewarding project is merely the beginning, not the end, of the work. The anger and pain in their relationship were important and needed attention. For healing to occur, it is crucial to help people see and incorporate their pathology without shame. The Smiths' anger and pain were approached as an understandable corollary of their deep connection and their intense competitive styles. Both they and the therapist developed a clear, appreciative view of their underlying competence, which altered their view of the problem, and freed them to alter the pathology cycle. To be free from their pathology, they had to befriend it and accept it as the best they could do at the time. Only then did the effort used to block it become available for creating new interactions and patterns. Mr. Smith would still be cold and critical at times. Both father and son had to see that as part of him, but not as all of him. Rather than pretending that he would not be that way any more, because he was now a great basketball teacher, the focus was on teaching both Mr. Smith and his son to challenge their old patterns respectfully. The same was true of Junior being rebellious and dismissive at times; it was not all of who he was.

This process is made easier when there is an awareness of the healthy components within the pathology itself. As Angyal (1965) writes:

> Tracing manifest disturbances to the acceptable motives generated within the neurotic framework takes one only halfway towards understanding them. This partial understanding fills the person with shame and guilt, which in themselves are not conducive to change. Real understanding traces the neurotic manifestation all the way back to its healthy sources. When the neurosis is discovered to be an approximation or a twisted version of health, the patient's outlook becomes hopeful. (p. 287)

It is this hopefulness that all therapy attempts to engender. A competence view enables the therapist to challenge a person's "twisted version of health" without fundamentally labeling or condemning the individual. One can challenge the *pattern* without challenging the person. Thus, the therapist could challenge Mr. Smith's cold, critical behavior as his pattern of unhealthy fathering, while at the same time acknowledging and supporting his strong commitment to and caring for his son. Rather than being mutually exclusive phenomena, they are viewed simply as juxtaposed and intertwined. The focus becomes *redirecting* the energy of pathology rather than eliminating it. Our friend Chad Glang has called this "finding the path in pathology."

Finding the Path in Pathology

The traditional psychopathology focus does not utilize people's natural motivational processes. It is aimed more toward moving people away from their dysfunction than toward their health. How then do we find the "path" in the pathology? How do we trace the manifest disturbance back to its healthy source? How do we combine a focus on pathological roots with one on competent undertakings?

The first element of integrating dysfunctional patterns and competence movement is the temporal orientation. A competence approach is oriented toward the future—what people are striving for, where they were headed before they got off track. One reason the psychopathology model offers little by way of a path out of the dysfunction is because of its time orientation. It is primarily based on the importance of the past and the ways that the past is reflected in and has determined the present. It is interesting, however, to question this idea. David Berenson (1992), for example, suggests that while people have always believed that the past leads to and determines the future, the reverse is also true: The future determines the past. A man robs a bank not because he was poor and deprived as a child, but because he wants to be rich as an adult. A woman cheats on her husband not because she saw her mother do it but because she wants to feel loved and special. The *motivation* is largely future-oriented; the *methods* and patterns for reaching what they are motivated toward often come from the past.

A psychopathology focus not only underestimates a person's health (or capacity to be healthy), but also is oriented toward the past and away from what may actually be motivating behavior—the future. So, in order to integrate pathology and competence, we hold on to the healthy motivations and try to jettison the maladaptive patterns. We work on competence in the present to get to the future we want, instead of just to undo the past with which we are stuck.

A second element in integrating competence and pathology is the belief that mastery and belonging are our fundamental motivations. Angyal articulated this best. He saw these two undertakings as the central, repetitive concerns that guide and energize us. It is a very different formulation from Freud's idea of sex and aggression, although near the end of his life, Freud also identified "love and work" as the important elements of a full and happy life. It is an expansion of White's (1959) work, which focused solely on mastery. Viewing the struggle for mastery and belonging as our core motivation enables us to view people as fundamentally seeking useful and productive outcomes, but sometimes getting lost along the way. A competence approach always tries to understand what a person is striving for, what hopes and dreams underlie the behavior.

A final element of this integration is the conceptualization of psychopathology as potential energy. For too long we have conceptualized psychopathology as something that has to be quashed or cut out. Angyal, for one, suggests otherwise. His conceptualization of people having within them two fully intertwined but competing systems—one oriented toward health and the other toward dysfunction—means that energy directed toward pathology does not need to be eliminated, but rather redirected so that it can be better utilized by the healthy system. Viewing psychopathology thusly is a natural offshoot of the assumption that people are fundamentally healthy and that pathological behavior represents failed or misdirected solutions. One strives then to find within people's psychopathology the underlying healthy urge (most often directly related to mastery or belonging) and redirect it toward a more successful outcome.

"Trying Too Hard"   Sarah and Tony waited to have a child because they wanted everything to be perfect. They had established their careers, worked the kinks out of their marriage, and built up a nest egg. But child-rearing became a cautious, tense project. They doted on their daughter, Jessica, and gave her anything she wanted; rarely did they say "No." Rather, they would

try to cajole her out of her bad moods or just tolerate them, assuming it was "just a stage" she would outgrow.

Things were fine until Jessica entered school. What they discovered then was that their perfect child was a perfect monster. She was a bully in class, uncooperative with both teachers and peers, and prone to tantrums when she didn't get her way. Sarah and Tony were devastated. Both their childhoods had been filled with isolation and loss, and they hadn't wanted Jessica to have to experience any of that; they were crushed that she was so unpopular and unhappy.

Although the focus for helping this family could easily be on the significant parenting mistakes Sarah and Tony had made and their own problems reflected in their child-rearing choices, that seemed to miss their strength. Clearly they were enormously motivated to do a good job. They valued parenting highly, and they had high hopes for Jessica's future. They would do anything to help her grow up well. The therapist needed to redirect this energy, rather than concentrating on their mistakes.

The therapist began by reviewing their goals for Jessica: Clearly what they wished most for their daughter was that she feel competent and secure. As she reviewed their failed attempts to make life perfect for Jessica, the therapist emphasized the good intentions behind them. Tony and Sarah, freed from defending themselves, voluntarily critiqued each point. They speculated about their own issues that gave rise to each parenting mistake, and they were fairly harsh on themselves. The therapist offered her view that their mistakes came from a lack of any healthy models. Their "overdoing" was not malignant, but was born of ignorance. But Sarah and Tony were quick to worry that it *was* malignant. They overinserted themselves into the equation again, this time as the worst parents in the world, instead of the best. The therapist pointed this out and was then able to help them make use of their pathological pattern. "The problem is not that you were deprived as kids and are trying to make up for it. The problem is that you're trying to be perfect. Because you both had to raise yourselves, you have too much faith in the importance of your input. Stop trying to be perfect [drop the method] and trust the power of your caring for your daughter [keep the motivation]."

With this map in hand, they responded very well to guidance

about healthy parenting and began to engage with Jessica in a much healthier way. By emphasizing her faith in their vision for Jessica and believing in their healthy motives, the therapist helped them to tolerate the distress of beginning to discipline their daughter. They were able to alter their patterns without feeling like they were abandoning Jessica, because the energy behind the failed attempts was still alive and well.

The focus of inquiry in more traditional approaches is on psychopathology as the fundamental inner disturbance of the individual. The focus of inquiry in a competence approach is the human spirit: How has it come through and what energy does it still contain for self-repair and healing? What work is the soul still doing on itself? What is the "path" in pathology?

When we approach people with a psychopathology lens, we look for the structural damage done to the developmental process. Is she fixated at a particular phase? Has he developed crippling anger? Is her guilt too great or his impulsivity too strong? It is an inquiry born of the disease model: "What is the illness?"

In a competence approach, the inquiry is not about what is ill or broken, or even about what is working well. Rather, the inquiry is mainly about what is *possible*. Our greatest interest in pathology is to see what healthy interests have been blocked or distorted, and the pattern of that dysfunction. We attend to and pursue what the person cares about or longs for in relationships and for himself. We are interested less in what is broken than in what was being pursued when it got broken.

A competence view of psychopathology, then, has several components. Psychopathology is only *one* part of the person, and is by no means the essence; psychopathology is intertwined with health and should be viewed as an underlying striving for mastery or belonging that has become misdirected; and psychopathology is potential energy that needs redirecting, not quashing or cutting out. Rather than focusing on the completeness of the pathological pattern and reifying it as a static disease entity, the competence focus concentrates on the *incompleteness* of the healthy wish. We try to capture the potential energy and use it to help the person complete the transaction in a healthy way.

We believe that the notion of psychopathology, with its implication of psychic disease, has been in many ways a destructive concept. We prefer to focus instead on the concept of *dysfunction*, which implies only that something does not work effectively or does not have the desired outcome. We see therapy as a process oriented toward restoring that lost function. We focus on helping people review their ideas of what they set out to master, and help them return to the journey.

five

CREATING A VISION

Where there is no vision, the people perish. . . .

—Proverbs 29:18

AN ELDERLY FRIEND of ours, Spurgeon English, once said that the secret to a happy life is, "Something to do, someone to do it with, and something to look forward to." It is a great formulation and pulls together many powerful themes. It also epitomizes the theme of a competence orientation to therapy. We certainly focus on having something to do, with our interest in competent behavior and proactive moves. We also emphasize the importance of "someone to do it with" in our attention to partnership and direct engagement. In this chapter, we focus on the question of having something to look forward to. A positive view of the future is an extremely important aspect of life. Though we live with the past, and in the present, a huge amount of our attention and effort goes into our future. What we have to look forward to and move towards guides our behavior constantly. The future, however, is the hardest of the three time frames to think and talk about because it is unknown. Yet, in some ways, it is the most important, since it is the one that can still be shaped. It is the repository of hope.

A vision of how we want our lives to proceed is vital to how we conduct ourselves day to day. We all have ideas about what is important and how to achieve it. If those visions are either too desultory and hopeless, on the one hand, or unrealistic and wishful, on the other, they cannot guide us to outcomes we care about. But most of us manage to maintain visions that balance aspiration and reality and keep us striving in a hopeful fashion. Whether we are looking to accomplish something specific at work or home in the immediate future, or trying to figure out a major theme for our lives, our vision of what we are shooting for is crucial. Consider the following scenarios:

Two 16-year-old girls both hate school and are considering dropping out. Both are of average intelligence, have similar social skills, and have limited support from home. Anna views school as boring and irrelevant to her future; her frequent absences confirm that. She plans to marry her boyfriend in a year, have two children, and earn money by keeping other children in her home. Her only hesitation about dropping out of school is that she has just learned that being a child-care provider requires a license and proof of certain skills; these skills are obtained most readily in the school's vocational classes. She's irritated by this news, but plans to find out if these same skills can also be obtained through a G.E.D. program.

Zoe thinks "school sucks" and skips often. When asked what she wants, she answers with what she doesn't want: school, a dead-end job, a marriage like her mother's. When pushed further for her goals, she talks about having enough money so she would never have to depend on anyone again. She thinks that if she is suspended one more time she just won't go back. She doesn't know or seem to care what she would do instead.

The two girls are almost indistinguishable demographically, but worlds apart in terms of their grip on life and, more specifically, their orientation toward the future. Anna has a vision of what is possible and what she wants. When her vision is threatened, she's activated. Zoe, by contrast, has a defensive, angry stance toward the world; she has no vision. She knows only what she does *not* want; her hopes extend only to not being miserable or dependent. Clearly she has enormous energy, but it is now bound up in her battle with the world. Without a vision she cannot connect that energy with a plan that can move her forward.

Traditionally, we would think about the differences between

these two girls in terms of their pasts. What enabled one to be resilient while the other wasn't? What resources did Anna have that Zoe didn't? In our more pessimistic moments, we might speculate that Anna's energy for the future was a defensive delusion, a way of avoiding the past. With few exceptions (Markus & Nurius, 1986), we fail to note the tremendous impact that having a vision has on behavior. And we fail to help people like Zoe create one when it has been lost.

Similarly, in therapy, a vision of where a client wants to move is crucial to both the client's and the therapist's conduct. The solution-oriented theorists (de Shazer, 1985; O'Hanlon & Weiner-Davis, 1989) have written extensively on the importance of a future orientation in therapy. For example, O'Hanlon and Weiner-Davis state that "In order to really prompt solutions, it is useful to develop a 'vision' or description of a more satisfactory future, which can then become salient to the present" (1989, p. xvi).

While we share their interest in the future, our approach differs from solution-oriented therapy in an important way. The solution-oriented approach does not emphasize creating a broad vision with the client of how they can be different. Instead, their focus is on developing a particular solution to a particular problem. While it may happen that, in the search for solutions, clients develop a more hopeful vision of themselves, we prefer to make developing a hopeful vision a priority in therapy. Such a vision seems to us critical to continued growth beyond the immediate problem.

The Vision Process

Many systems of therapy use the first session(s) to evolve a shared vision of what the problem is and what improvement would look like. Our interest in this is not so much to develop a particular goal or solution, but to stir people's interest in what is possible, to raise their sights. We want to increase people's energy for discovering and pursuing what matters to them. We are less focused on a single vision or goal than on the larger idea of developing a vision mechanism.

What does vision mean to people? How do people think about their sense of the future? When we speak of vision, we do not mean anything as clear and specific as a particular plan or intention. Those may contribute to a person's vision, but we are more interested in an individual's sense of *possibility*. We want to expand people's repertoires more than we necessarily want to add a particular skill. Resuscitating the hopeful sense of future is of greater importance to us than creating a specific future. Often a specific competence-building endeavor with a client is as much a model for proactive engagement with the future as it is a goal-oriented effort.

Possible Selves

The work of Helen Markus and her colleagues (Markus & Nurius, 1986; Markus, Cross, & Wurf, 1990) has helped us to think about both the importance and the nature of people's sense of themselves in the future. They refer to people's visions for themselves as their "possible selves" and view this as a significant component of hopefulness (or dread). Possible selves are people's conceptualizations of themselves as they could become, would like to become, or are afraid of becoming (Markus & Nurius, 1986). Their findings about the impact of one's sense of the future on behavior have three important implications regarding the need for creating a vision in therapy: (1) A positive vision can help one cope with a current crisis; (2) a vision of oneself in the future provides cues about the path and/or methods for getting there; and (3) a sense of what is possible acts as an incentive for present and future behavior.

Regarding the first, how a positive possible self helps one to cope, Porter, Markus, and Nurius (cited in Markus & Nurius, 1986) found that, when faced with a crisis (such as loss of a significant person), there was little difference between people reporting a good vs. a poor recovery in terms of how they described themselves in the present; both identified that they felt lonely, weak, underachieving, etc. However, the two groups differed significantly in their view of themselves in the future. Those who had a positive perception of themselves in the future (motivated, intelligent, creative, etc.) coped much better in the present than those who did not. Thus, a positive hopeful vision of the future appears to improve present functioning.

Markus and her colleagues also concluded that a vision of oneself in the future provides clues about how to achieve wanted change. Knowing what the desired future looks like helps people design a path from the current state to the desired future. Markus et al. state that, "The construction of possible selves allows one to experience a *contingency* between one's now self and one's imagined future self" (Markus, Cross, & Wurf, 1990, p. 208). The common expression, "If you don't know where you're going, any road will take you there," is exemplary of this: Knowing where you are going makes choosing the right path much more likely.

Finally, a sense of oneself in the future can act as an incentive to present behavior. How we want to be can guide what we do now to bring that about. When certain current self-conceptions are challenged or supported, "it is often the nature of the activated possible selves that determines how the individual feels and what course the subsequent action will take" (Markus & Nurius, 1986, p. 961). People with no vision of their future — no possible selves — obviously cannot use such a vision to organize their present behavior. Their behavior will be much more random than that of someone who aims for a desired outcome.

Markus and her colleagues' elaboration of the specific mechanisms by which a vision of the future alters the present highlights how important creating and nurturing a sense of possibility and vision of the future may be in therapy. Bandura (1990) adds one other important variable to this equation. He has delineated the importance of people's beliefs about their efficacy in determining behavior and how those beliefs affect attention and learning. If people do not have a sense of the possibility of mastering a task, they will not pay attention to the cues and feedback that could help them to master it. A mother who has given up on teaching her difficult child to cooperate, for example, will not notice the impact of her actions (positive *and* negative) as much as the mother who is still hopeful about the outcome. If there is no expectation of future success, there will be no awareness of present functioning. If people believe they are capable of managing or mastering a task, they tend to exert more effort and persevere longer. Bandura (1990) has determined that it is the "resiliency of self-beliefs," not lack of self-doubt, that is the critical variable.

Life is filled with difficulties, setbacks, and failures; it is a robust sense of self-efficacy and belief in the possibility of positive outcome that enable one to overcome them.

Developing, supporting, and expanding people's vision mechanism and their sense of what is possible is, therefore, a critical component of therapy. Having a vision of oneself in the future can offer protection in the present, hope for the future, and cues about how to proceed. Loss of a vision and a sense of negative possibility can be equally powerful in stagnating growth and change. When our clients come in shrouded in pathology and dysfunction, they offer us a negative view of their possible selves. It is the therapist's job to search for more, to uncover their underlying competent strivings and their belief in positive possibilities. The challenge is to see past the obvious flaws while honoring the real limitations. To do that the therapist must strike a balance between hope and reality.

Hope and Reality

Hope is an important subset of vision to which we have alluded often. Like some of the other elements we wrestle with in this book, it is not usually a part of serious thinking about therapy. Yet it is a crucial variable in life, and its loss can be a devastating blow. "Feeling hopeless" connotes a deep and even dangerous level of personal distress.

Hope can be a superficial concept and sometimes appears primarily to be a positivist wishfulness that avoids or disguises painful reality. For instance, hoping for things seldom makes them appear unless it leads to effective action. Paul Tillich distinguished between two kinds of hope: "Hope is easy for the foolish, but hard for the wise. Everybody can lose himself [sic] into foolish hope, but genuine hope is something rare and great" (quoted in Snyder, 1991). We are interested in what makes up genuine hope, the kind of hope that can alter people's outlook and behavior in a fundamental way.

A further analysis of hope suggests that it has two parts: agency and pathways (Snyder, 1991). The agency component of hope is "a sense of successful goal-directed determination"; the pathway component "involves a successful sense of planning to meet one's goals" (Snyder, 1991, p. 287). We would translate these two components into our frame of reference as courage and competence. The idea that hope depends on a clear determination to get where you want to go is what we call courage. Knowing what to do to get there is synonymous with competence.

Both agency and pathways have been shown to be crucial elements in effective therapy. In a meta-analysis of psychotherapy studies, Barker, Funk, and Houston (cited in Snyder, 1991, p. 299) found that, "a sense of agency improves psychological functioning, and that the additional sense of pathways doubles this improvement." Hope depends on agency and pathways, or courage and competence. To a significant degree, creating a vision in therapy depends on hope.

But hope for what? What Tillich calls "foolish hope" is common among people. To be useful, hope needs to be balanced with a somewhat realistic assessment of what is possible, or it leads only to disappointment and bitterness. We have all seen the boy who hopes to become a rock star by listening to Led Zeppelin albums and never gets his electric guitar out of its case. If he invests energy in the wish, but none in the necessary pathways, he will end up with nothing but disappointment. When people treat success as an on-off mechanism and hope it will be flicked on for them, they are almost always disappointed. Hope needs to be for something more or less attainable, and it needs to lead to action. Stretching one's self is important; as Browning said, "A man's reach must exceed his grasp, or what's a heaven for?" But stretching also needs to involve some assessment of what's possible.

In helping people develop "genuine hope," we try to capture their striving and shape it, by helping them move to realistic pathways. Sometimes this involves making use of strengths they possess but have not recognized. At other times it requires helping them to develop abilities that they did not have before. People ignore their strengths as often as they ignore their weaknesses. Directing them towards their unclaimed capacities is as important as helping them develop pathways where there have not been any.

Hope can certainly imply unnecessarily rosy views of the future, but we find that people as often have unnecessarily hope*less* views of themselves. By the time people get into therapy, they are often so embedded in their problem and their concern about it that they have a very distorted perspective. "I completely fall apart when my parents come to town," a young woman says. The facts are that she gets somewhat anxious, especially about her mother's tendency to second-guess and criticize her. But the last time they came to town, she functioned well and even had people in for dinner on a work day without getting unduly anxious. She does *not* "fall apart," and she needs to challenge that vision of herself. If she truly does fall apart, the task is different. In either case, the fundamental task of the therapist is to help the client determine a healthy vision of where she wants to go—whether that involves creating new skills or recognizing existing ones—and then to act in the present to bring that about.

In helping people to change, it is critical to understand what they were hoping for, their sense of possibilities, and what strengths and abilities they feel they can call upon (if any) to get them there. A competence approach works to engender a strong sense of positive possibility, of hope, while remaining respectful of people's sense of negative possibility and their realistic limitations.

"Starting Over"   Stanley, 25 years old, came for individual therapy because his older brother had refused to allow him contact with his 11-year-old niece until he received help. Stanley had been reported to Protective Services for "acting weird." He had been sneaking up on his niece when she was dressing, coming into the bathroom when she was bathing, and getting an erection whenever she sat on his lap.

Stanley also presented to the therapist as weird and frightening. He was unkempt and had difficulty maintaining eye contact. He spoke of his sexual arousal around his niece as "thrilling" but also upsetting. He dreamt that he might mutilate someone and had, as an adolescent, dismembered a cat during a particularly heavy drug use phase. Stanley also revealed that he had been thinking of suicide because his niece was the most important person in the world to him, and he feared he might hurt her. He had lost any hopeful vision of himself as a functional person or family member.

The therapist asked Stanley to share his history and listened for how and when Stanley's healthy urges had become warped. Stanley revealed that he was the younger of two sons, by 12 years, from an upper-class family with an abundance of money, but no love. His father died when Stanley was a toddler, and his mother remarried a man who "got weird" as he got older. Following the stepfather's lead, Stanley and his mother were expected to shed their clothes as soon as they entered the house. His stepfather never actually molested Stanley but constantly pushed the limits of acceptable behavior. He would slap Stanley on the rear whenever he passed by, tease him about erections, and roughhouse with him naked. Since the family was also very reclusive, it was not until adolescence that Stanley sensed his family's behavior might be different, and he coped by retreating into drugs. The idea of behaving differently in the family seemed impossible to him; he could only run away. He completely cut off from his parents after high school and only reconnected with his brother five years before starting therapy. With his brother's help, Stanley had given up drugs and found a job. Stanley's greatest attachment, though, was to his niece. It was the distant hope of a good relationship with her that moved him to put some real energy into therapy.

Reviewing Stanley's history, it was not hard to understand how his underlying urges for mastery and belonging became warped. In his family, any kind of intimacy was sexualized. He had no model for being loved, much less for appropriate intimacy, so he never developed any comfort in that area. When he now felt tenderness towards his niece, he experienced it sexually. While these feelings confused and upset him, they also excited him with the same ambivalence he probably felt growing up. How, then, could he be helped to map a different direction for himself?

The therapist offered Stanley a different vision. First of all, Stanley was told that it was his *family*, especially his stepfather, and not him that was most disturbed. They had failed to provide him with an appropriate model for intimacy, and he had been doing the best he could given that void. He was told that how he had been raised was indeed "weird," and it was sad that no one had labeled it as such for him. His own recognition of their weirdness and his desire to retreat from it after adolescence was underlined as a strength. Therapy was structured as a continuation on that path of seeking normalcy and disconnecting from the warped atmosphere he was raised in.

Secondly, he was invited to learn how to develop a model of appropriate and inappropriate intimacy. The therapist started by asking Stanley to share in detail the pain of his past. Through these memories, they developed a map of what was and was not appropriate intimacy on the part of his parents. He remembered a housekeeper they had had for several months who had refused to disrobe and seemed capable of saying "No" to his father. She was fired. He was helped to identify with her, to see both the inappropriateness of the adults' behavior and the victimization of a young boy. In this way, he was encouraged to remove the shame as he reviewed his past and to see himself more sympathetically, in much the same way the therapist saw him. Contextualizing his past behavior also enabled Stanley to distance himself from it somewhat, thereby creating enough space to envision other possible selves in the future. If he wasn't all weird, what else could he be?

Thirdly, Stanley was encouraged to appreciate his brother, both for insisting that he must do better and for offering his niece the kind of care and protection that was so sadly missing during Stanley's growing-up. With his brother's protection in place, Stanley was helped to discriminate when his feelings of tenderness for his niece became sexualized and to learn to convert them back to tenderness. Stanley could not alter his behavior in a single leap. He practiced this in small steps with the therapist prior to seeing his niece and then with his niece, again under carefully controlled circumstances.

Finally, Stanley was reminded that this would be difficult work and would require courage from both him and the therapist as together they learned not to become overwhelmed by his pain and horror. The therapist had to remind herself that it was important not to minimize the horrors Stanley had experienced. The vision for Stanley needed to be respectful of his health and his pathology. His past had left him with some grave problems. Yet a desire to fit in better and function successfully had also survived. Through courage, determination, and a different vision for himself, Stanley could resolve his horrors and find a different path than the one he had been on.

Reviewing the focus of this treatment plan, it is easy to see how critical creating a vision of Stanley as being more than just weird was to the work. When Stanley entered therapy, neither he nor his brother initially had a vision of his positive possible selves. Rather, they were both stuck in seeing only his past, present, and future dysfunction. What the therapist offered Stanley was a hefty dose of hope and reality: the hope that there was more to him than just weirdness and the reality that his horrors were deep but could change by small, well-managed steps. The healthy concomitants that the researchers describe as resulting from having a positive sense of oneself in the future—better coping with current crises, seeing new information, motivation for changing and persevering longer—could begin to be utilized by Stanley.

Creating Vision in Therapy

Therapists' Vision Mechanism

We have talked in some detail about the importance of developing the client's vision mechanism. As the last case exemplified, it is also important that, as therapists, we develop our own mechanism. Our ability to maintain and pursue a vision of where we want to go in any given case is critical. While some would say that the therapist's vision is irrelevant, we believe that a healthy sense of what a family or individual needs to be working towards is a vital contribution by the therapist.

In fact, the lack of such a vision is often the death knell of a case; it frequently signals the therapist's loss of hope for a family. If the therapist has no vision of where the family can and needs to go, it often belies his sense of their being unmovable. We usually have the least vision for the families we feel least good about. Caring and vision are closely related. A hopeful vision for someone is often a specific offshoot of affection for them.

Another principal task of the therapist is being able to compare his vision for a case to that of the client and to see which is more appropriate and has more possibility. Sometimes, people know what they need, and we merely help them to get it. Often, however, people come to therapy with a misreading of what they need. When they do, we must be able to provide a vision with more possibility.

"The Would-Be Mourner"   A 47-year-old man appeared in a family therapist's office asking for antidepressants and citing the need to do some grief work. His wife had died two years previously of cancer, and he had been "joyless and in pain" ever since. He looked the part. As the therapist began to inquire into the story, however, he was impressed that the man seemed to have grieved in a relatively healthy and direct fashion. He reported that he thought of his wife with pleasure and affection and missed her; he had "few regrets" about their life together. But he continued to mourn her and felt he really needed to "work through" his feelings about her.

After learning more of how he had gone about mourning, the therapist asked his thoughts about dating again or remarrying. The man flared visibly and said, "My God! It's barely been two years!" As the therapist inquired into his reaction, it became clear that the man could not begin to think about his future without great anxiety and concern. While he initially cited guilt and feelings of betraying his late wife, the issue soon focused more on his lifelong anxiety about enjoying himself and having fun. He had always enjoyed life by taking care of other people. Now he was embedded in a view of his future as empty and isolated.

The therapy never really dealt with his late wife or with his "depression." In fact, that would have been a retreat from the real issue. Instead, the therapist invited the man to focus on his avoidance of his future and his difficulty thinking about his own needs. As he began to figure out what he wanted, and to pursue it, the symptoms of depression disappeared. The man's vision of himself had been as a crucible of loss, grieving, and investing further in his past. Had the therapist followed that logical and theoretically sensible vision, his struggle with knowing and developing his own future might never have come to light. Through the therapist's lead, he developed instead a vision of himself as someone who could enjoy life again and experiment with "following his bliss."

If we are to lead, we must gain our clients' trust. This is especially true when working to create a vision with a client. It is vital that the client trust the therapist enough to believe and accept her vision. If a vision is provided too quickly or glibly, and the client does not trust where it comes from, it will not be helpful. Many of us object to motivational tapes ("You are fantastic and can do anything"), because they are unconnected to us. It is a universal vision, not an individualized one. To be powerful, the client must feel the therapist knows all of him—past and present, strengths and liabilities—and the vision must be connected to *his* underlying strivings.

Pattern vs. Person

How does one create a vision that honors the past but is more oriented toward the future? How does one move closer to a client or family without becoming overwhelmed by their flaws? Many personality theorists have focused on distinguishing between a person's real self and his other selves as a way of trying to work with this duality of health and pathology. Schwartz (1988), for example, has developed a therapeutic approach that capitalizes on our "multiple selves" and the energy that is generated when our polarized parts are helped to deal with each other.

The model that we have found most helpful is one proposed by Steve Greenstein (1992), which distinguishes between clients' "patterns" and their "person." Their patterns are the habits that they have developed over the years, probably useful at one time, but now limiting. Their person, on the other hand, is their underlying healthy "real self," that is, their healthy impulses toward mastery and belonging. From the earlier example, Stanley's pattern was to sexualize his feelings of intimacy. However, what he really wanted—his person—was to feel loved and lovable, but he had no healthy ideas about how to make that happen.

When therapist and client learn to distinguish between the pattern and the person, several things happen. Separating the damaging patterns from the healthy self is consistent with our conviction that people are basically healthy and that pathology is an adaptive attempt gone awry. For example, being able to distinguish between Stanley's pattern (of getting "weird" or sexual when he felt love) and his person (someone craving attachment and acceptance) enabled the therapist to develop a vision with him that utilized his underlying energy in a more healthful direction. This process of actively distinguishing between a client's pattern and his person enables the client to see himself more hopefully.

In Stanley's case, the therapist made the distinction between pattern and person overt. The client can then look at his pattern with less shame because it is does not define him; it is not his essence. Distinguishing between the two conveys the sense that he has a choice about how to be. He can be encouraged to think about alternate ways of being that more closely fulfill his underlying urges. Distinguishing between pattern and person enables the therapist to form a collaborative relationship with the person while challenging the pattern. The therapist can be ruthless with the pattern at the same time that she is gentle with and respectful of the person (Greenstein, 1992).

We have found that people respond positively to the acknowledgment of their multiple facets. They readily make the distinction between their different parts and are relieved when the therapist sees more to them than their pattern. Often, they know that the healthier part is there; they just don't know how to trust it and let it lead. Helping them to develop a different vision of themselves and where they want to go enables them to let the healthier part lead.

But it is not always easy to distinguish between someone's pattern and their person. In order for us, as therapists, to do this we must be able to see our clients and their struggles with what Stephen Levine (1987) calls "soft eyes." "Seeing with soft eyes" conveys the importance of opening our hearts to people and viewing their pain, anger, or pathology in a way that enables us to move closer to them. But moving close to someone is not enough. It must also include the generation of hopefulness and movement. Satir (1988) was a master of this. She was able to sit comfortably with people's pain, in part, because she never lost sight of their potential for movement, healing, and change. She had a hopeful vision for people and invited them to adopt it as well.

"The Necrophiliac"   Sam, an extremely intelligent 16-year-old, had a long history of acute anxiety. The only child of older, anxious parents, he had long been the recipient of their cautions, fears, and worries. Rather than knowing how to see their concerns in context, however, Sam tended to amplify and exaggerate them. His parents requested help because Sam seemed increasingly depressed and isolated. In an individual session a few weeks into

therapy, Sam revealed that his isolation was partly a result of his growing conviction that he was a necrophiliac. He found himself obsessing constantly about sex with dead girls. And he was intrigued and delighted by the horrified reactions he got from classmates, especially girls, when he told them of his interest.

Sam provided a detailed history of both his difficulties and strengths, which suggested that he had struggled with many of life's tasks. He had difficulty going to school as a kindergartner, changing schools in fifth grade, and, most recently, moving on to high school. At each stage, he developed some kind of disorder (germ phobia, anxiety attacks), which both represented his anxiety and delayed the transition. His primary sense of himself was as a "nerd," poor in social skills and unable to develop friendships. But Sam also knew that he was intelligent and creative. He liked being an expert at things and spent many hours mastering new computer games. He was excited about being a necrophiliac because it made him interesting and different, albeit unapproachable to his peers. He was determined to be an intriguing nerd, at least.

When faced with anxiety-arousing challenges, Sam's pattern seemed to be to magnify the difficulty of the challenge and denigrate his ability to master it. Rather than experience what he saw as "certain failure," he would pathologize himself and his behavior. It was in this context that his budding necrophilia needed to be understood; it was part of his pattern, but not his essence.

The therapist's job was to create a vision with Sam that honored the reality of his anxiety while also building on his wish to be seen as lovable. Sam needed a vision that reoriented him toward a healthy path. The energy and excitement he felt about being a necrophiliac needed to be redirected to the underlying healthy task that had become too anxiety-arousing for him — interpersonal sexual interest. Because of his terror and anxiety about failing (or perhaps about succeeding) on the normal path, he was trying to master sex backwards.

In order for Sam to move past his pattern of avoidance and isolation, the therapist needed to help him develop a more healthful and hopeful view of himself without completely stripping him of his wish to be intriguing.

Sam was told by the therapist that she was glad to work with him on his necrophilia, but since that was an advanced sexual orientation, they needed first to work on what Sam knew about regular sex, sex with live girls. He was reminded that one can't advance to college level material until one has finished high school!

Sam was nervous, but interested, since he knew little about sex. The next several weeks in therapy were spent educating Sam on the fundamentals of a relationship with a girl, specifically, and of sex, in general. With this focus, the therapist related to his healthy interests and not to his unhealthy pattern of being a strange nerd. His pattern of scaring people away with his symptoms was also undermined. Sam's interest in necrophilia dropped away as he became more relaxed and comfortable with his feelings about intimacy and sexuality. He began to be optimistic about the possibility of a normal relationship with a normal girl. He even started to plan how to act more normal with his peers, and to learn healthier ways of being intriguing. The key to developing a more hopeful vision with Sam was understanding his "necrophilia" in the context of his underlying longing for mastery and belonging. He longed to be an expert at something; he just needed a healthy focus for that energy.

Escaping the Ruts

The human tendency to get stuck in ruts is frequently what causes the loss of vision. Clients despair (which literally means to lose hope) and get trapped inside a world view that is narrow and restrictive. The therapist's ability to see beyond the rut the client feels herself in is a crucial part of therapy. The importance of that ability accounts for elaborate training in objectivity, transference, countertransference, and so on. Empathy is helpful, but the therapist who begins to see the world only through a client's eyes, will feel narrowed in with no vision of where to go, becoming useless to the client. Like parents who cannot help a child with a problem because they feel it too acutely themselves, such a therapist will have limited success. Successful therapy depends on the therapist's vision being less limited than the client's.

Reorienting the Path

Creating movement in therapy depends on having the ability to envision multiple pathways to a client's desired future. Often clients come to us because their path to a goal is blocked and, in the process of trying to bulldoze through, they have lost their vision. All they can see is what they are not doing or cannot do. Or they get anxious about their chosen path and, in abandoning it, abandon their vision for themselves as well. In order to help them, we, as therapists, need to have a sense of the multiple pathways that they can follow to get where they want to go. When one is blocked for whatever reason, the therapist can then provide redirection to a more manageable path.

Being able to conceptualize multiple means to an end is slightly different from reframing, a useful technique that uncovers multiple meanings or possibilities in a situation or behavior (Watzlawick, Weakland, & Fisch, 1974). Reorienting the path is the ability to hold a clear or broad enough vision of an end state so that if the client becomes anxious, resistant, lost or just stuck, several different ways of getting there can be offered. Like reframing, envisioning multiple paths is a skill that requires being able to think expansively and creatively. Following is an example of this skill in a non-therapy setting.

While watching a young boy during a swimming lesson, one of us noticed that the carefree attitude of his first day was replaced by second-day terror. He got in the water, but no amount of gentle coaxing could separate him from the wall. In fact, as the teacher persisted in cajoling him, he got more scared and began to creep along the side of the pool to escape.

I then watched, awestruck, as the teacher creatively changed this into a game of chase, until they were both halfway around the pool. In the process, of course, the boy became increasingly relaxed in the water and was using the wall less for clinging and more as a way of traversing the pool to "escape" the teacher. When the teacher then invited him to be his partner in chasing the other children, he eagerly jumped into the teacher's arms and they were off. Terror and resistance were nowhere to be found.

The teacher's brilliance was in turning the boy's resistance into a path related to the original goal, learning to swim. He accepted what was offered and, by switching paths, slowly turned this energy in a more productive direction. Erickson (Haley, 1973) understood this well. When teaching about the importance of using people's inherent energy, he used the example of a man trying to change the course of a river. If he tries to block the river, it will either go over or around him. "But if he *accepts* the force of the river and diverts it in a new direction the force of the river will cut a new channel" (p. 24, italics added).

This is a skill that is particularly needed when working with adolescents. Driven by their anxiety, they are often resistant to finding workable paths, even when they do not particularly want to be resistant. In the process, the resistance becomes ensconced and they lose a sense of where they were headed in the first place. They are helped when the therapist can both tolerate their noise and adapt their movement in a way that reconnects it to their original goal or vision for themselves. Vision is crucial to adolescents, but they often fight it.

Reorienting the Vision

It can be particularly difficult to help those who, in addition to personal traumas, also have a long family history of hopelessness and despair. Their history of despair may overcome our commitment to a useful vision. Often economically deprived, the family heritage may include failure, loss, and abuse of various sorts. The family may have seen a string of therapists, school counselors, and court officers, among others. It is hard not to feel despair even before they are halfway through their story. Their entire lives, not to mention their immediate problems, seem overwhelming.

Sometimes, the therapist's job is to become more respectful of the family's struggles. This may require an accurate assessment of what the family needs most. Helping them obtain more appropriate shelter and clothing may need to be accomplished before tackling school problems, for example. Or it may mean providing enough outside support, structure, and safeguards that they can begin to relax their vigilance and make use of the therapy. Building a competent base to work from is crucial; we must go as far back as necessary to establish that working base. Sometimes, a vision of a better future must be deferred while the present is made livable.

At other times, the therapist's task is to help the family challenge how they have conceptualized their struggle, to help them reorient their vision toward a path that has a greater likelihood of success. Too often, family members get stuck waging a battle they have no chance of winning. Rather than talking them out of the battle, or coaching them to fight an unwinnable war, it is often more productive to reorient their vision toward another, more achievable goal.

"The Peace Plan"   Jill, 35, was a brittle diabetic with long-standing fears about independence and success. She had "married the wrong man," and soon returned to her hometown with her infant daughter. She was a very attentive mother to Jody, now age six, but always in the larger context of not being attentive to her own health. She had frequently slipped into diabetic comas, leaving Jody to call her grandparents for help. Following her release from the hospital, a battle would ensue over the caretaking of Jody. The grandparents were in their late 60s and did not really want to do active parenting again, so they would eventually return Jody to Jill, but not before being terribly critical of her. This pattern could be seen as one precipitant of Jill's stress. It was now beginning to take its toll on Jody as well. She frequently misbehaved with her grandparents; this was taken as a sign either of poor parenting or poor grandparenting, depending upon who you asked.

The therapist met individually and collectively with all the family members and eventually adopted Jill's vision that this time, with support from the therapist, she would "win the battle" of who was in charge. Plans were made for how she would take better care of her health and become more responsible for Jody. A key component of this move for independence was lining up friends to provide child care should she need hospitalization. Jill arranged it and promised to call them should she begin to feel ill. With this in place, the grandparents would not need to be involved, and Jill would "win."

The plan was sabotaged during the next medical crisis. Jill ignored warning signs and slipped into a coma. Rather than calling the designated friend for help, Jody called her grandparents. They took Jody home for a week, even though Jill was only in the hospital for four hours. Jill was furious with her parents for not following the plan and was ready for a showdown, including cutting off any further contact with them unless they acknowledged her as the boss. It was only then that the therapist realized how flawed Jill's and her vision for change had been.

Because of the brittleness of Jill's diabetes, she was always going to have medical emergencies and, thus, need support to parent Jody. And the grandparents were very much Jody's first choice as substitutes. Given this, Jill was never going to "win," if winning meant not needing help from her parents. Her vision for herself needed to be reconnected to her underlying striving to master parenting rather than toward defeating her parents. She needed to direct her energy away from trying to win an unwinnable game and towards getting out of the game entirely.

In order to do that, a different vision was created with Jill. She was asked to take it as a given that she was in charge of Jody. It was no longer a battle; she was the mother and always would be. Next, she was asked what a competent mother would do if she needed help with her child. Jill figured out, with some trial and error, that such a mother would probably set up with the helper what help was needed, give directives to the child about how to behave when with the helper, and be appreciative of the helper's efforts. Jill was invited to follow this map in her interactions with her parents. Rather than continuing to feel defeated at tasks she could not accomplish, a different path was outlined that had a greater likelihood of success. The vision was reoriented toward her behaving like a competent mother, rather than striving to defeat her helpers.

At the next family session, after some preparation with the therapist, Jill began by voicing her appreciation for all the support her parents had provided her. She recognized and praised their invaluable contributions as grandparents. While they sat in shock, she then instructed Jody on how she expected her to behave when at her grandparents', since the grandparents were doing Jill a favor by helping out. (In the past, Jill had been secretly pleased at Jody's misbehavior with the grandparents, because it was a sign they were not winning.) She made it clear to Jody that the grandparents deserved respect.

In this new form of taking charge, Jill was able to accept help without being defeated. The grandparents were able to give help that was honored and appreciated. Jody stopped getting double messages about behaving. Redirecting the vision toward peace, and providing a new path for reaching it, gave the family a more hopeful sense of where they were trying to go.

Creating a vision with clients does not eliminate or even shorten the work of therapy, it merely provides a more hopeful, healthy structure in which to contain it. It channels the energy in a way that empowers the client and reunites him with his possibilities. Its function is to create a view of the desired future in a way that helps to organize the present more usefully. Everyone has some vision of the future, and that idea will infect the present, positively or negatively, usefully or destructively.

Skill at pulling a workable and positive vision out of the problems we are presented with is crucial in a competence approach, precisely because of our belief in a proactive posture. If there is no vision, it is impossible to take a proactive step. By the same token, however, the concept of vision cannot be taken out of a larger competence context. A therapist should not try to develop a vision in the abstract. A vision depends on understanding and accepting the past and the patterns of dysfunction; it depends on testing clients' capacity for proactive behavior, and finding out what they are capable of and have done before; it depends very strongly on partnership. It's not a castle in the air to be built on clients' behalf, with forced occupancy the next step. It is the natural result of a mindset that believes in always moving towards mastery and belonging.

six

COURAGE

Why don't the psychologists ever talk about courage?

— *Charles Darwin*

COURAGE IS A VARIABLE that few therapy approaches deal with. As therapists, we often find ourselves needing to enhance the client's ability to undertake difficult action, and courage is a necessary part of doing so. People get stuck in their patterns and problems and lack not only the strength to try something new, but sometimes any idea of what to try. To figure out where they want to go instead, and how to get there, requires courage. A critical component of a competence approach to therapy is an appreciation of this attribute, both for clients and therapists.

There is much about ourselves that is difficult to change. Our psychological makeup, poorly understood as it is, is not a highly movable feast. We all have to do the best we can with the combination of inborn and acquired patterns that we develop. Doing the best we can with what we have means several things. First, it means knowing (or finding out) our unhealthy patterns and vulnerabilities. We must also know (or find out) our healthy side and what we really were pursuing as we developed those patterns. Then, it means finding and organizing our strengths and resources. Finally, it requires us to use those strengths and resources to move away from our unhelpful patterns towards where we want to be. In short, finding our maladaptive patterns, under-standing where they come from, and changing them, are our tasks.

These are often frightening and difficult tasks. Maladaptive as they may be, our patterns are at least known to us, well-worn and molded like an old pair of slippers. To try something differ-ent, even if it could be better, means risking loss, pain and failure. To change, we often have to acknowledge that, in some fashion, what we were doing was not the best thing to do. We also have to let go of secondary gains gleaned through our bad habits—the attention of being the "sick one," the fun of impulsive or self-serving behavior, the power of an explosive temper. Finally, we have to stretch ourselves and come up with a new pattern, a different way of being that raises our hopes but has no guarantee of success. Changing our maladaptive patterns often feels like we are out there on our own. Anxiety is inherent in growth and change, which is why they require courage.

Courage has many different meanings and implications, but the most important one for us is precisely the meaning that Webster (1968) provides: "the attitude or response of facing and dealing with anything recognized as dangerous, difficult or painful, in-stead of withdrawing from it." This same ability to face and deal directly with something difficult, confusing, or unknown is the core of a competence approach. The concept of taking competent action to "make life work" has at its core the idea of "facing and dealing with" problems. Being willing first to see and then to change what is unproductive or misguided takes courage. It is often easier to hang onto what is known and safe, even if it is not what one wants or hopes for. Courage has as much to do with the spirit and the soul as with the psyche. It is an element of the relationship between therapist and client that is difficult to look at directly, but crucial to the kind of work to which we aspire.

The Client's Courage

People develop several kinds of courage in therapy. One is the courage to face their true feelings, both positive and negative, and to deal with them honestly and directly. That sounds simple enough, but we all grow up with many layers of defense and self-deceit between our most real selves and the selves we put out for public and even personal scrutiny. We learn to evade parts of our selves in many ways, and we may fear self-confrontation even in the relatively safe environment of therapy. A pathology focus in therapy may serve to exacerbate that fear. So, for people to turn inward in an objective fashion, to move past the layers of defense, and to challenge some basic structures, takes a lot of courage.

For clients, the hard work of therapy often lies in honestly addressing what they feel most strongly. It is not feelings that get us in trouble, but *fear* of those feelings and of the suffering we imagine will follow if we really let down our guard and experience them. "It is not power that corrupts, but fear," as Kyi (1991), a Nobel Peace Prize winner, has said. It is our defenses, not our impulses, that bring us pain and misery. So the primary courage in this world is the courage to feel directly and honestly what it is in our hearts, both positive and negative, that is guiding our behavior. When that journey is undertaken, therapy has real promise.

If, as is often the case, the outcome of that work is that some specific changes are needed, then a second kind of courage is required: the courage to change. From leaving an abusive spouse to disciplining an unruly child, even obviously necessary and appropriate changes often call for courage. If those things were easily or simply achieved, the changes would not require therapy. Most of the kinds of changes that therapy leads to require "dealing with difficult things instead of withdrawing." But those difficult things are often nothing more than a direct engagement with reality: "You need to leave before he abuses you again" or "You've got to get your child under control."

Why do these obvious changes, which most anyone could see the need for, require courage? In part, we embed our avoidance of them in our sense of weakness. "I can't make it alone," people say, or "I can't stand how he acts when I discipline him." Each of these ideas is predicated on a sense of being unable to tolerate the distress of doing it differently. We get attached to our patterns of compromise and retreat, and we come to feel dependent on them. The process of letting go of our patterns and trying something new may seem impossible, terrifying, or confusing. However logical the change looks, there is some combination of loss, guilt, and fear that makes the change distressing.

It is at this juncture that the therapist must *encourage* the client — which means, literally, to provide with courage — to continue the journey. As has been suggested by Podvoll (1983), "a quality of courage is not only necessary for recovery but is the nature of health itself" (p. 190).

"Bonnie's Werewolves"   The family seemed chaotic and unruly. In the wake of their parents' recent separation, the 9- and 12-year-old boys were fighting each other and their mother nonstop, and mom was depressed and avoidant. But the clear, identified problem was the 14-year-old daughter, Bonnie. Hypermature, intense, and obnoxious, she ruled the family. She refused to go to school, slept all day, and watched TV all night, in spite of mom's feeble protests. When challenged by her therapist about her domination of the family in the second session, she listened in a bemused way and then hissed through clenched teeth, "You are *way* . . . out . . . of . . . line." Though her delivery was chilling enough to raise everyone's anxiety, there was also a palpable terror in her bearing. The therapist resolved to stay unafraid of her, for her sake and his. Later on in the session, she implicitly offered a pseudo-truce by being conciliatory and "explaining" her symptoms, but the therapist pushed on, feeling a more honest connection could be made. Towards the end of the session, she struck again, roused to anger by the therapist's unwillingness to back off when she offered a truce. As her hostility level escalated, he tried to stay with her, less scared of her anger than before.

Bonnie: You don't understand *anything*!

Therapist: I understand that you want to run the family and avoid yourself.

Bonnie: I don't! You're *so* stupid! That's not what I want. I just want to be left alone.

Th: To have your way and avoid your feelings.

Bonnie: No! Just to protect myself, and feel OK. [Here's a glimmer — she's off the attack, and looks confused for a minute.]

Th: Protect yourself from what? What are you afraid of?

Bonnie: Nothing . . . (*She tears up for a second, then regains the attack*) Just leave me alone!

Th: It's not nothing. I think you're scared to death. This is all cover up.

Bonnie: (*Starting to cry*) I cannot *stand* the feelings I get! I just want to get the werewolf off my back. [She had mentioned the "werewolf" before, but I hadn't gotten it. Now it was clearer.]

Th: The werewolf is the feelings you get if you can't protect yourself?

Bonnie: I hate it, it is *so awful*! You don't understand how those feelings are.

Th: No I don't, but I want to. And your mom wants to. You've been hiding from those feelings by being a tyrant, and it's *not working*. Have the courage to try something else: Let your mom and me in on this with you. We'll help you with those feelings.

Bonnie: You don't know how bad they are! (*sobbing*)

Th: You're right. But I know they can't be as bad as the terror you live in, protecting yourself the whole time by fighting for control. Try to let go.

Bonnie cried for a long time and then took the therapist's hand when offered. In the sessions to follow, she continued to cautiously let the therapist and her mother in to the feelings that she had been fearful of for so long. Each time that she would get feisty and nasty, there was the implicit understanding that she was fighting off terror; they were just stand-ins for "the werewolf." With this understanding, it became easier for both her mother and the therapist to go soft and not battle the bratty behavior. As a result, the brattiness dissipated faster and faster. She began to take pride in letting the feelings in instead of keeping them out. The fundamental balance shifted in the family as mother followed the therapist's lead and moved *in*, rather than closed down, when Bonnie got imperious.

The greatest single advantage of experience as a therapist may be the ability to move more quickly and more directly to the place where courage fails the client and the fearful pattern takes over. The retreat into a distress pattern born of fear and confusion is an enormous backwards step in any case. The ability to block that *and* provide courage to go forward is a contribution. The therapist's resolve to not be scared off by Bonnie and lending her some of my courage to face the "werewolves" enabled her to deal with them more directly and honestly herself.

But how do you restore courage? It is not just letting feelings in until fear dissipates and courage ascends. Fear dissipates as one develops competence around the fearful areas. Courage does not spring up full-blown where it has been lacking. Rather, it grows incrementally as the area gets strengthened and filled in with some sense of mastery. As Bonnie began to let herself and her mother see and understand the feelings she dreaded, she was able to deal with them directly for the first time. They were appreciated, understood, and made safe. Then, the difficult work of mastery in those areas could begin.

In tracking the case of Bonnie, one of the observers behind the one-way mirror asked, "How do you know if the mother can help Bonnie? She's depressed, she's characterologically passive, and she's self-obsessed. What makes you think she can help her daughter?" It is a classic question—and a classic error. If we ask this question based on a psychopathological view of people, our answer will likely be, "She can't help her daughter." If, however, we respond from a competence orientation, we look for the place in mother from which she can *best* respond and help her daughter. We try not to see the patterns she is habitually in as complete limitations, but to find a way out of them—or better yet, a way to use them to do something different. We try to see past the patterns to the person: She has much more to offer than her pathological patterns, and we need to tap into that instead.

In this case, the mother was supported to meet her daughter halfway and help her feel less afraid. The therapist's task was also to lend courage to the mother in order that she might challenge her pattern of avoidance as well. The mother had a difficult time doing it. She *was* self-absorbed and frightened of her daughter's intense feelings. The therapist went slowly with her, lending courage, helping her to master her own anxiety and to not block Bonnie's fears by getting lost in her own. Strong support for mom to match her daughter's courage helped her to approach Bonnie and her "werewolves" more directly.

The Therapist's Courage

An issue of the *Family Therapy Networker* contains a short story by Mary Hedin (1990) entitled "The Mean Kid." The central character, a 13-year-old boy, has had a life full of rejection and abuse. His mother is a prostitute and drug addict, his father is long gone, and the boy has been rejected by four foster homes. His new foster mother is a middle-aged widow who, when her husband was alive, had taken in foster children as substitutes for the children they could not have. Her husband had died three years ago and she had not qualified for any children since then because she would have been a single mother. But Social Services was desperate for a placement for this young man, so she agreed to take him.

In the story, there are several nice examples of the foster mother using a competence approach in her interactions with this boy. For example, she notices him stealing money from her and confronts him. But rather than taking a hardened position that will lead to his running away, she connects with his underlying healthy striving. She recognizes and agrees that a boy his age needs an allowance and offers him one. But because he is "a mean kid," he rejects the offer and boldly tells her he wants more.

The string of near misses continues. Neither is quite able to connect solidly and rewardingly with the other. He wants her to claim him more, so he introduces her to a friend as his mother; she laughs and corrects him. She develops with his teacher a plan for him to pass at school; he will not follow it. Finally they each go too far. He fills her favorite vase with dirty rocks; she explodes, slaps him, and gives up. Later that night, he hangs himself. Incredibly saddened, she comes to understand that her real failure was her lack of courage with this boy. As she says to herself, "The poor kid, the poor scared kid. You knew all the time how scared he was. You were just too proud to love a kid mean and ugly like that" (p. 68).

We often get stuck with our most difficult clients at just that point: We don't have the courage to keep caring. We want to think that with a simple new technique, a new way of questioning, or a different use of language, we can master any particular problem or type of pathology. But, in reality, our stuckness is less often a failure of technique than a reflection of our not having enough courage to "love a kid mean and ugly like that." It requires courage to open our hearts to a difficult case.

The underlying idea of a competence orientation involves being willing to take people as they are and find in them the roots of their best and most effective functioning. To follow those roots wherever they lead is potentially very difficult. If we are to follow people's passion, we have to be prepared for some wild rides. It is not a sanitary endeavor. A person's passion often goes directly through the middle of his or her rage, love, craziness, and confusion. It requires us to take serious and respectful interest in the most real parts of them, whatever those parts may be. If we are truly willing to find and develop their passion and their competence, we will have to take some chances.

Therapists, therefore, also need courage. The therapist is expected to lead into areas of difficulty and danger and to find her way effectively amidst the client's anxiety and her own. The hope (or expectation) of a solution provides further tension and pressure for the therapist. Beyond merely surviving strong and discordant emotional interactions, she is supposed to use them to make things *better*. She is expected to know how to guide people to a safe outcome from a direct and perhaps even explosive version of the problem.

We don't want to hope for a safe outcome, however; we want to pursue a really good outcome. We want to aim high and hit our target. Needless to say, we are frequently unsuccessful. But the process of aiming high—of asking ourselves, what is the best possible outcome here, and how can we try to bring it about—tests the therapist's courage every time. Like any reach, the therapist's grasp for a really good outcome can fail; a lot can go wrong. In some ways, the most amazing thing about therapists is that they keep trying, keep risking being wrong, in a profession where falling far short of the ideal is routine. We're either very brave, or very slow learners.

"Breaking New Ground"   Ken and Penny were at an impasse after 20 years of marriage. The older they got, the more they felt different from each other, and the less each appreciated the other's uniqueness. Ken was more distant and fuzzy than Penny, who

seemed to have come to therapy to work. Part way through the second session, the therapist said to Ken, "I want you to be completely honest with me. Will you? (He nodded.) I think you came here to drop Penny off with me, so when you leave she'll have someone to crash with. I think you want to play at therapy, then make a run for it. Could I be right?"

This so startled Ken that he could not even think of a denial. After a very long, awkward silence, he merely said, "You could be." The therapist went on, "If that's what you really want to do, have the guts to do it honestly and don't play games. If you want to continue here, you have to be willing to risk getting back into this relationship in a way that works. What do you want?" Ken responded, "I don't know. I honestly don't." The therapist said, "Thank you for being honest. You need to think hard about this. Don't come back unless you're willing to keep on being honest, whichever way it goes." Ken agreed, and the session ended.

They called for an emergency appointment two days later. Ken had hardly slept in the two intervening nights; they had talked and fought more or less non-stop. An affair had been revealed by Ken, a near-affair by Penny. Years of avoiding each other had been broken. When they came in, Ken said, "I feel like we've talked more in the last 48 hours than in 20 years. I don't really know Penny—although I may be beginning to. I certainly don't know myself. I'm *so* confused. I need time away to think by myself: I want a separation."

The therapist was stunned. What had sounded like a prelude to some real work suddenly became a bowing-out. He decided to challenge it: "I think it's a mistake, Ken. What can you think about alone that you can't think about with Penny—and/or with me?" Ken waffled and rationalized. He assured the therapist and Penny that there was no one else and no other agenda. The reason finally came out that he felt inadequate dealing with Penny at this level of intensity. It wasn't confusion, it was fear. "She seems to know what she wants," he said, "And I'm grasping at straws. I have *no* idea where the hell I'm going. I feel so stupid, I can't face her." The therapist responded, "But Ken, that's your pattern—not knowing where you are going. (This had been discussed before—Ken felt he was in corporate lockstep with no real satisfaction in his work.) You've always kept your own counsel because it scares you to be confused in the open. It doesn't look like it has been good for you; you don't work these things out well alone. How about trying something new? Let Penny help you work it out, let me help you. It's time to come out with your confusions. Don't retreat and repeat your old pattern of hiding from it."

Ken listened to this, looked at Penny, and started to cry. "She can't love me if she sees me stumbling around . . . ," he began. Penny cut him off: "I can't love you if you *won't* stumble around with me, dammit! You've never let me see any of your confusion. I *like* your confusion! I'm confused, too! Don't run away. We either learn how to go through it together, or we quit. No more neat exteriors over crappy insides. He's right. We either learn how to hurt and be confused together, and help each other through it, or we pack it in." They stayed in therapy and made real progress.

Therapists often pull out at the point at which this one dug in. There are times when clients are pulled in profoundly unhealthy directions by old patterns, and the therapist has the opportunity to let them go with no blood on his hands. The temptation to do so is strong; it gets us out of sticky situations guilt-free. They did not show, or the husband wouldn't come, or the identified patient acts out in a particular way; a host of rationalizations can justify therapists' quitting. "I did my best," we say, "but they just couldn't do it." Sometimes, that is true. But very often, it is precisely a new version of the pattern that has gotten them in trouble. Rather than calling it for what it is, the therapist rolls with it, and gets off the hook.

Ken could easily have been given room to pull back and have a separation, but it was entirely isomorphic with his whole ineffectual pattern. This needed to be challenged in order to break the pattern. To help Ken have the courage to do something different, the therapist needed to have the courage to challenge him and risk failure. While there was much more novelty and movement possible from blocking Ken's retreat, the therapist also risked anger and blame. As therapists, we need to be willing to have the courage of our convictions and to take clear positions.

Using Ourselves

The variables that make people fearful and cautious are actually relatively few, and they seldom divide us from our clients. The things that trouble them are most apt to be the things that trouble us: intimacy, anger, self-worth, connectedness. So as we get near our clients' terrors, we can usually feel our own hearts quicken as well.

When our hearts quicken like this, we are usually in danger of working on our issues instead of the client's—countertransference, in a word—and we have to be careful not to act out on people under the guise of courage. In general, the rule for therapists has been to quash their countertransferential feelings and to react as little as possible when they get near these intense feelings. That robs the therapist of a large and potentially vital energy source, however. When both client and therapist are in an area of strong feeling and reactivity, there is the opportunity to make considerable progress. But to do so takes courage and clarity. We have to know ourselves and our own issues well, and we have to be willing to move into difficult waters.

"Laying Down the Sword"   While working with a very tense and authoritarian military father, whose 15-year-old daughter was fighting him tooth and nail, I (Edith Lawrence) found myself becoming angrier and angrier with him. I could certainly identify with the daughter and found his approach demeaning and unreasonable. I wanted to go after him. A moment's reflection reminded me, however, that everyone in the world had gone after him, and it never worked. It wasn't going to help; it was just going to make *me* feel better. If I was going to get him out of his pattern, I was going to have to get out of mine.

Instead of going after him, I went towards him. As much as it infuriated me, I tried to find out what he was working on via his authoritarian approach. I assumed he was genuinely interested in his daughter. I reached out to him the best I could in an attempt to break both his pattern and mine. The hardest part of this was to try and find out where he was right, and underline that, when I mostly wanted to prove him wrong.

As I pushed myself to know him more fully, I began to trust in his fatherly feelings. I asked him to teach me about the pain and sadness that would move a father to do what looked like attacking his daughter. I had to suspend judgment (not easy at this point) enough to really hear his answer. I had to take what I got, and not have a particular thing I needed him to say. In order to teach me about himself, he had to move away from the attack on his daughter (not easy for him, either) to help me see where he was. In the process, he began to show me the caring I had tentatively trusted was there. We both learned to drop our agendas and do something healthier. And we got to a clearer and much better understanding of him and his relationship with his daughter.

Developing Courage in Therapy

Where do the questions of courage for client and therapist intersect? What draws us to their loss of heart? What leads them to come to us for encouragement?

We believe that it is the process of providing courage to each other through partnership and collaboration that makes therapy work. Therapists, in general, are people who are actively interested in the process of gaining courage—their own as well as their clients'. (Michael Elkin is fond of saying that "Therapists are just people who need 8 hours of therapy a day, but don't want to pay for it.") It is partly our ongoing interest in where and how people find the strength and creativity to carry on and do better that draws us to study the process of therapy.

The personal collaboration toward finding strength and courage is what makes therapy work. Courage, though finally an internal variable, is much more possible between collaborators than it is in solitude. There is something profoundly heartening about going on a difficult quest with a trusted partner. This is why the therapist-client match is so critical. It is not the cognitive match that makes the difference as much as the emotional pairing of people who can encourage each other and risk the journey together.

It is also important to remember that the road to courage is paved with competence, not simply with challenge. Competence and courage co-evolve. It takes courage to think about growing, changing, and facing inner demons. At the same time, the journey must be made up of competent steps. Courage and competence rise and fall together. This we see as the heart of therapy—the interplay between a client's courage and competence and the therapist's conviction that both are givens. As the therapist works with the client's initial courage, the courage to enter therapy, he must support and develop that fortitude by uncovering underlying competence.

How does a therapist encourage a client? What conditions are necessary before acting courageously becomes an integral and supported part of the therapy? Functionally, there appear to be two fundamental aspects to the process: acceptance and action.

Acceptance

The first task is acceptance of the problem and the fear that accompanies it. "Fearlessness may be a gift, but perhaps more precious is the courage acquired through endeavor, courage that comes from cultivating the habit of refusing to let fear dictate one's actions . . . " (Kyi, 1991). What a wonderful concept: refusing to let fear dictate our actions. We all react out of fear and avoidance much more than we might wish or like to admit. A competence approach enables us to go toward people and their problems, to understand them well enough to see their healthy as well as their unhealthy roots. Being able to see both aspects enables us to remove the shame from them.

Shame and courage are orthogonal. When we feel shame in connection with something, we are usually disempowered by that shame. We retreat, cover up, and settle for whatever will get us away from the discomfort of it. Shame promotes hiding and self-protection. It does not promote self-acceptance. Courage requires openness, vulnerability, and direct engagement. To engage with something, we have to see it for what it is and accept it. When people understand and accept their fears and concerns, the hold of those fears and concerns is loosened. Our belief and interest in the underlying competence of people's motivation actively undermines their shame.

"Making Amends"   Rhonda appeared for therapy looking guilty and wretched. She alternately blew up at her two girls (nine and seven), and ignored their inappropriate behavior. Strangely, she seemed to ignore the more egregious behaviors and blow up at the lesser ones. The therapist, a relative novice, quickly began

to see her as a poor mother and started to try to shape Rhonda up. Not surprisingly, she got nowhere.

The therapist was encouraged by her supervisor to understand Rhonda more and try to change her less. She was encouraged to find out Rhonda's thoughts on parenting and what she wanted for her kids, what she was striving for. Initially, Rhonda anxiously avoided the question; finally, in tears, she said that they had been abused by their father (now absent) for several years. She had not known how to stop him since he also abused her. Rhonda felt ashamed and guilty about this failure on her part and wanted to be sure they were never abused again.

Thus, Rhonda became confused and anxious when she was really angry with her daughters. She blunted her angry reaction to their worst behavior, and chose lesser infractions for which to reproach and correct them. After appreciating her eagerness to atone for the husband's abuse, the therapist helped Rhonda see that her reversed reactions actually *undermined* her daughters' learning. The therapist and Rhonda conspired openly about a new and better format for letting her daughters know she felt badly about not protecting them. Rhonda decided to apologize directly and seek the girls' forgiveness, instead of merely acting indecisively out of guilt. This became the first task of the therapy: Rhonda's direct approach to her children with the issue of not having protected them adequately. She was able to do it in a positive and even proud way, since she saw it as a useful step in getting to be a better mother instead of as a painful exercise in self-flagellation.

Most problems have an equivalent of this process, which we tend to think of as the "caring side" of the inadequate behavior. Rhonda's confused reaction to the girls was actually a misguided attempt to make up to them for her earlier failure—a kind of perverse gift. (Overindulgent parents and overly strict parents alike believe they are doing what their children really need.) People's ineffective or unsuccessful behavior is most accessible when they realize that the therapist's interest in it is benign and designed to promote acceptance more than criticism or blame. No theory of insight actually espouses criticism and blame as positive factors to be sought, of course. But many psychopathologically-oriented therapists get stuck in the criticism/blame loop and don't get back to helping the client make a proactive move. If Rhonda hears only, "So you act out your rage at yourself and your ex-husband on your children and repeat the inadequacy of your earlier failure with a new version of failure . . . " as the therapist's input, she will have no way to make use of the interpretation. She then probably *will* experience it as blame and criticism, and it will deepen her sense of shame and inadequacy, instead of helping her move towards something better with her girls.

It is difficult, if not impossible, to accept and make use of new meanings if they are purely negative, *because people don't recognize them*. Rhonda cannot accept and work with a view of herself that is built entirely around acting out unconscious rage, with no place for her very real love for her children, her sadness about her failure, and her wish to be a good parent. She can accept the therapist's word for what is wrong with her, but she will probably not be able to work with it very well. It will not feel like *her* in a way that sparks useful action.

Action

Useful action is of course the second aspect of how courage develops in therapy. Once the process of acceptance and incorporation has been established (not completed—it never is), the second element of developing courage follows. It is what Kyi (1991) refers to as "the courage acquired through endeavor . . . [by] refusing to let fear dictate one's actions." When one acts on a new awareness, and goes from altered idea (insight) to altered behavior (change), an important sequence of events occurs. The pattern is interrupted, and the sense of hopelessness is diminished. As new data are produced and (hopefully) processed, a different sequence(s) can be set in motion; the person gains the role of actor, initiator, effector, with all the impact that has. Awareness alters one's sense of past (how it got this way) and/or present (how it is now). Action alters the sense of future: where to go from here.

When we speak of action in this sense we are talking about the process of taking competent steps that help get us where we need to be. Not just action per se—doing something for the sake of doing it—but healthy, effective, competent behavior. In therapy this usually builds directly on the awareness that precedes it. Most healthy action is built on new data that alter what is possible or desirable. And when people have the knowledge and do *not* act on it by allowing it to affect their behavior, they move away from courage, not towards it. The very basis of tragedy, from the Greeks on, is knowledge that does not lead to action. It is not just a wasted opportunity, it is a significant step backwards. Hamlet, paralyzed and unable to act, at his own peril, represents the loss we suffer when we do not use knowledge to move forward in a healthy and courageous way. When we let our actions be dictated by fear, we lose more than time and opportunity.

"Going to Texas"   Crystal, 14, was brought to therapy by her divorced parents. She had been involved in an escalating pattern of problems for about a year: staying out late or overnight without permission, sexual involvements with several boys, drinking, and skipping school. In the last two weeks, these behaviors had increased in intensity, culminating in a 48-hour absence. The parents, Don and Gina, had finally reached a critical level of concern. Though divorced for over two years, much of which was spent in bitter fighting, they had gotten together to deal with this new crisis. Bringing Crystal to therapy was their first cooperative decision.

Don and Gina had been marginal parents for most of Crystal's growing up. Although they were now both in recovery, they had been alcoholics for most of her youth, and Crystal had learned to expect little from them. In the first session, Don, Gina, and Don's girlfriend, Barbara, took seriously Crystal's self-destructiveness and committed to do whatever was needed to help her change these patterns. The three adults cooperated well to bring more structure and control into Crystal's life, and within a few weeks she began to calm down a little. She was helped to deal more honestly with her peers and to make hard but healthier choices for herself. There was an eagerness to do better behind her "bad girl" front. Taking care of herself in appropriate ways, learning to say "No," and not protecting her parents from her feelings were central themes.

Six weeks into therapy, Gina and Crystal (who lived together and were the primary focus of the therapy) dropped a bomb. Don had called the night before to say that he would be moving to Texas in a couple of weeks to take a new job. He was excited and had presented it as "good news" for all involved. Crystal told the therapist about it in a tone that was resigned but not too upset. The therapist, by contrast, saw it as a painful renewal of the pattern of undependability and loss that Crystal had had to endure from her parents most of her life. Here, as the family was just beginning to do a good job giving Crystal the nurturance and guidance she needed, dad was pulling out. Abandonment was not what she needed at this point.

The therapist pursued Crystal's feeling about dad's leaving. Crystal was very sad but so used to protecting her parents that she had difficulty voicing this. Rather, she was pulled by her old pattern of rationalizing and excusing them. While she was able to share with the therapist the hurt and sense of betrayal, she had no idea how to deal with her father about it, except to close down.

This is often a place where therapists get stuck with clients. They are not quite ready to act, yet not acting will result in a tremendously important missed opportunity. They need to take a step that they are unable to take alone. It takes courage and clarity from the therapist to help clients take advantage of a fleeting opportunity such as this while, at the same time, making sure it is the client's agenda, not his own, that is being followed. Traditionally, our training as therapists has been excellent at teaching caution in therapy. However, a more effective approach often involves courageous action on the part of the therapist.

With Crystal's permission, the therapist asked the parents and Don's girlfriend to a family session to focus on the move. She began the session by appreciating the courage both parents had shown not only in acknowledging and changing their alcoholic patterns but also in moving past their marital bickering in order to provide Crystal with the support and guidance she so desperately needed. The therapist then challenged Don's interpretation of the move and his commitment to his daughter.

Therapist: This is really an important juncture for this family. You three have been doing a great job of being there for Crystal, and she has worked hard because of it. But now, Don, you are planning on leaving her. She has just been getting used to your protection, guidance, and support and now you're taking it away. For financial reasons, you may have to leave, but you owe it to her to tell her the truth. You need to take responsibility here for bailing out on her at a bad moment. Don't dress this up as a great deal—for Crystal, it's another abandonment.

Don: But I have to have a *job*! I don't make enough here, and I will in Texas. She'll be better off.

Th: Maybe financially, but what she needs emotionally is her father. You weren't there for her when she was growing up because of the alcohol. You've just rediscovered her, and you've told her she could count on you. Maybe you have to break that promise—I don't know. I do know that you need to be honest with her and call your moving what it is: abandoning her.

Don: "Abandonment" is pretty strong. I resent that idea.

Th: Yes, it's strong, and while I'm sorry it offends you, it's the truth. Your daughter needs your support and guidance desperately as she tries to make healthier choices for herself. It's hard for her, and she can't do it alone.

Don: Don't I have a life, too? Can't I do what's best for me?

Th: Of course you can, but you need to *acknowledge* that you're doing what's best for you. Don't ask Crystal to be happy about what is really sad for her. Don't pretend it's for her. Tell her the truth, Don. She deserves that from you. She deserves your honesty. She deserves your fathering.

Don: (*long pause during which he begins to cry softly*) This is hard for me, Crystal. I don't know how to do this. (*long pause while crying*) I'm so sorry I'm leaving you. You *do* deserve better. I want to be your father and have you count on me. I need help to do it better, but I *really* do want to be your father. And I want to learn to be honest with you.

Don and Crystal worked hard on their new relationship until he left. He became much more honest with her and supported her doing the same. At eight-month follow-up, he was still calling regularly on Sunday mornings, and Crystal had come to depend on him as one of her chief supporters.

In this situation, the therapist was confronted with a choice:

making the father's exit comfortable, or using it to take a major step forward. The latter course—taking action with regard to Don's position—was more difficult but a much better path for both Crystal and Don. Don's actions had been dictated by fear. By challenging his fear and helping him to reconnect with being a father to Crystal, his avoidance of pain was replaced with a real chance to grow. Action of this kind often requires courage on the part of the therapist, and then, if the therapist succeeds, on the part of the client. It is usually easier to take a less active and direct stance, but it seldom yields as much growth.

Courage is a difficult concept to talk about; it is not always what we expect it to be. As with the famous definition of pornography, you know it when you see it. For that reason, we cannot program or plan courage very easily, especially across cases. Our goal is to help people to take honest, useful, and developmentally appropriate action. Part of the therapist's task is to see where the client needs to gain courage to take such action and then to support that work. Sometimes it seems obvious, sometimes entirely obscure.

Campbell's idea that the hero's journey is the journey inward, whatever the external metaphoric journey, is a guide. When we help people develop useful action, it is usually not the external aspect of the action that is crucial, but the internal one. For Rhonda, it was less important what she said to her girls, or what they heard, than what she said to herself by making the speech to begin with. When we help couples enter into a deeper, more powerful dialogue with each other and play their weak and painful suits openly, we are often less moved by what they admit to their partner than by what they admit to themselves. In that sense, courage is usually a personal journey.

As therapists, we are taught caution and circumspection, but not courage. That is certainly appropriate in terms of the order we learn things in; "First, do no harm" will always be good advice. But it is vital to think sensibly about bringing courage to therapy as wisdom and experience are gained. Therapy itself shows a model of courageous engagement with the world. Courage in therapy depends, in the final analysis, on the therapist's willingness to ask much of her client—and at least as much of herself.

PARTNERSHIP

Relationships . . . how one gets to the mind by going through the heart.

— John Thompson

WE HAVE RETURNED OFTEN in this book to the ideas of mastery and belonging as the two overriding motivations to which we all respond. We have focused heavily on mastery in pursuing various forms of competence, but have dealt only partially with the idea of belonging. Yet, in some ways, belonging is the heart of the operation. Relationships that work well and in which we feel truly connected to another person (or people) are vital. They are also very often what mastery is designed to produce. Most competence, in the end, has interpersonal rewards. It is in the limelight of good interpersonal relationships that our competence is most enjoyably viewed.

The very existence of therapy is a tribute to the power of partnership. Why would anyone go to a complete stranger and pay considerable sums of money to talk about his or her most painful and distressing thoughts and feelings if partnership were not a powerful process? The vital importance of sharing a difficult endeavor with a trusted cohort is hard to overstate. When one feels shaky or distressed, retreating into isolation generally does not help. Finding a friend one trusts and working on the problem with them generally does.

Collaboration

What are the advantages of such a partnership? There are numerous reasons we pull together with others whom we trust at such times. First, it provides a reality check. It is hard to see ourselves or our dilemmas accurately alone. Next, it provides courage. The more frightening anything gets, the more desperately we hope not to face it alone. Even if there is no actual additional protection, only a partnership, it is still vastly more comforting than going it alone. And if the other person can really help with the difficult endeavor, he or she is doubly powerful as a partner. Third, partnership provides motivation. All of us know the experience of trying harder and pushing ourselves farther when there is someone besides ourselves involved. Both pride and concentration are enhanced by sharing the task. At the same time, the partner for whom we are trying harder can also provide direct support. Appreciation, encouragement, challenge—there are various ways that trusted partners draw out the best in each other. Finally, partnership enriches both success and failure. In success, we have someone with whom to celebrate; in failure someone with whom to commiserate and recover. The natural pull to pull together is powerful and important.

We take the issue of partnership very seriously in our way of working. A competence approach depends on a high level of connection between therapist and family members. The steps of a competence approach, especially developing a vision and having the courage to move proactively, cannot be undertaken at a safe distance from clients. The very process requires an engaged, personal relationship that pulls on the therapist as much as it pulls on the client. Much of the client's courage and competence comes from feeling the therapist alongside her. We see family therapy as a shared journey, not as a carefully managed cruise that we send clients on.

The vagaries of partnership and collaboration are difficult to detail. How they are like affection, and how they are different, are both important but difficult to spell out. One of the questions we have learned to expect from Steve Greenstein when we seek his consultation on a case is: "What do you love about these people?" It is often the key to finding a way in to a level of collaboration that can make a difference. If the answer is, "Nothing," then we are not joined with them. We do not have enough appreciation of how they came by their problems honestly, and we do not see past those problems to their strengths. We believe that every problem has a caring side, but that side will remain imperceptible until one finds a way to care about the person.

When we do know what we love about the client, it often tells us where to build our vision and where to challenge for change. The process of finding people's healthiest, most rewarding and heartening qualities is a vital aspect of partnership. Health-hunting requires a strong level of engagement; for us, pathology-hunting occurs most readily when we are least connected.

Time and again we have found that when we push ourselves to find something we like about a client, a change occurs: a change in us, in our client, and in the relationship. The very process moves us to see clients in a new way and to feel differently about them. In order to find what we like about someone in an honest and nonsuperficial way, we have to move in closer to them and understand them more profoundly. People's flaws, while remaining visible, become less consuming. When we open ourselves fully to people, we see more readily how their missteps, more often than not, emanate from good intentions, albeit misdirected ones.

The process of being seen more fully also changes the client. All of us find it a blessing when someone chooses to see our flaws not as our essence but in the context of our health and strivings. We feel less shameful and defensive and, perhaps, more hopeful. So, too, do our clients. Seeing past their pattern to their person reminds clients of their underlying competence and conveys a sense of hope.

Finally, the change that occurs in the relationship when a real partnership exists is significant. No longer are therapist and client stuck in a cat-and-mouse game, wrestling for secrets. Rather, it becomes collegial and collaborative. If clients do not feel they will be branded by their mistakes, but are encouraged to see in them their healthy strivings, they are more likely to be forthcoming.

This is when magic can occur; this is when client and therapist together can stretch themselves further than either could go alone. It is often when new vistas are opened for both.

"Bring It on Home"   A young couple, married three years with no children, came for therapy after the husband's brief affair was discovered by the wife. The wife was in great distress. Above and beyond the natural devastation of the affair, it deeply offended her fundamentalist religious principles. The husband was contrite in a formal sort of way. He said the right things, but it felt to the therapist like he was merely taking his punishment. The wife's pain, by contrast, was easy to respond to. The therapist soon found himself strongly allied with her and increasingly angry at and alienated from the husband. He presented the case to a supervisor with the question, "When is it okay to push for a divorce?"

The supervisor quickly saw the therapist's dilemma. He was allied with the wife, but had not gotten beyond the husband's most superficial exterior, and now did not want to. When the supervisor asked how and why the affair came about, the therapist had only the wife's perspective. The husband had never made any contribution to that discussion, but meekly accepted her version of it. The therapist was encouraged to find out what the husband thought the affair was about. More generally, he was to find some things he could really like about the husband (and thereby stop playing the role of "angry father-in-law" to him). The therapist objected to this quite strenuously, feeling like this would be coddling the victimizer, but agreed to try.

The therapist saw the husband alone. He was surprised to find that the husband had a story that made sense and had a heart to it, even if the affair itself was wrong. He had grown up in a demanding and restrictive household where he had to be in bed by 9 p.m. even as a high school senior. Since he had not known how to challenge this directly, he had developed a secret life of fun and excitement (drinking, smoking pot, occasional sneaking out). He had learned to separate completely his responsible behavior from his playful, rebellious, acting-out side.

This pattern had continued in his marriage. He played on numerous sports teams, relishing both the games and the post-game beer sessions. The more he enjoyed it, the more it appeared to him that his wife disapproved. He had become more boyish and irresponsible over the three years of marriage, and she the reverse.

As the therapist began to feel connected with the husband, he could now ask less critically if being boyish was really what the husband wanted. The answer was "No"; he felt as trapped in this pattern as he had felt in having no fun. He recognized that he had his wife in the position of an angry parent, with little chance of their ever having fun together. The therapist helped the husband to look at the destructive (and self-destructive) consequences of taking his pleasure privately. They focused on breaking down the wall between his two parts. He also supported the husband in teaching his wife to be more playful so that they could have some fun with each other. The idea was initially shocking to the husband, as he could hardly imagine her loosening up. But as the therapist helped the husband to deal with his pattern and his unfinished business with his parents, the husband felt freed to begin to relate to his wife differently.

When the therapist had joined the system on the wife's side, there had been no room for movement. Now, the therapist could help the husband to be more direct and involved with his wife. He could challenge the husband's pattern of "misbehaving child" and refocus the couple on learning to have more fun with each other. When the therapist risked getting to know the husband's health as well as his pathology, his feelings about both partners and about the case changed significantly.

"Cherish Your Impotence"

One of the most painful realizations of a career in family therapy is that we do not really have much power or control. We can run the sessions and try to steer in useful directions, but our ability to do so depends on many factors that we do not control at all: the clients' cooperation, their creativity, the alignment of circumstances, pure chance. What we can do is help people make the best use of both their external and internal resources. As Carl Whitaker often says, "Cherish your impotence. It's the only tool you've got." The concept of "healthy indifference" allows us to engage clients actively and intensely without being so invested in the outcome that we rise and fall with them. It is possible to care about people without adopting them. We try to invest in the process of therapy, rather than the outcome. And we try not to fool ourselves that we control either process or outcome.

Many of the cases in this book have turned on bits of luck and good timing. The adolescent boy in Chapter 2 made a 180-degree improvement on the strength of Uncle Mario's serendipitous arrival on his chopper. The epileptic girl in Chapter 3 benefitted greatly from the fact that the end of the school year presented major opportunities to go public with her search for fellow epileptics. Stanley, in Chapter 5, was helped enormously by his brother's loving and firm mandate to get better. From a position of partnership, a therapist has a better chance to help the client notice such possibilities and take advantage of them.

Some clients, of course, are more willing or able than others to trust us and let us in. For those who have difficulty trusting, we may need to be patient. But we may also need to be courageous enough to join with them in a way that conveys that we are safe. Although that may include appropriate self-revelations by the therapist, that is not always or even often the case. What is critical is communicating to the clients in whatever way is necessary that our pursuit of a connection with them is based on caring and respect. There is an old saying that saints are just sinners who keep on trying. In the same vein, the best therapists may be just good therapists who happen to be really skilled at creating partnership, and thereby give themselves more chances to succeed.

The cases we have presented here have been cases where we did the best we could, and the clients responded with the best they could. We were not geniuses, nor they paragons of health. But it was enough to initiate movement and growth in a way that was fulfilling and self-sustaining. Often, it seems, the result of a good partnership is that the whole is greater than the sum of the parts. Ideas and plans develop in partnership that would not have occurred to either therapist or client in isolation. Similarly, both clients and therapists have patterns of retreat, loss of courage, rigidity, blindness, and brain-lock. In a good partnership, we pull each other out of these ruts and keep the process going.

Long ago, Freud wrote that one needed to "make the patient a collaborator." He said, "It includes those healthy realistic aspects of the patient-therapist relationship whereby the two parties influence one another in such a way as to arrive at common therapeutic goals" (quoted in Thompson, 1987, p. 87). We think a competence approach pulls for and magnifies the healthy, realistic aspects of the therapeutic relationship. While the therapist may have more training in and tools for developing and monitoring the work, at its best therapy must truly be a partnership to have the kind of powerful movement we think clients are seeking. As Peggy Papp (1984, p. 25) has noted, " . . . the artistry and magic do not exist in the therapist but between the therapist and the client." Good clients make good therapists make good clients.

"Stand by Us"   A young couple came to therapy to try to decide whether they would get married, after nine years together, or break up. Every time they had been close to deciding to marry, they would suddenly become mired in a massive fight pattern that would ruin everything and start them towards splitting up. Back and forth, for nine years.

In therapy, the therapist pulled hard on them to work through their terror of closeness and commitment. He developed a strong relationship with each one, and used it to help them move out of old ruts and relate in new ways. But they continued to see-saw: move closer, panic and pull apart, break new ground again. About five months into the therapy, the therapist suddenly hit his limit. After a new round of approach-then-run, he threw up his hands and declared himself convinced that they would do this forever. "We have our answer," he declared. "We've really tried hard, but the results are in. You need to work on saying goodbye and realizing you're not going to make it. Sometimes a clear goodbye is the best thing." He was sad, but so frustrated with their inability to break out of their pattern, and his inability to make the changes stick, that he felt this move was best.

The couple came to the next (termination) session with a large box in hand. They said to the therapist, "We understand why you're discouraged, but you're wrong." With that they opened the box and gave the therapist a tour of their life. From their first photo together to mementos of their many high points, they ran through the richness of their history as a couple. The therapist protested, but they good-naturedly waved him off. "You need to see how much there is between us," they said. "We want you to believe in our future as much as we do!" The therapist relaxed and entered into the playful spirit of the show-and-tell. Surprised by their determination, he soon became willing to be convinced. But he said they would have to work harder on following his lead out of the ruts they were in and stop indulging themselves in their ritual fights. They agreed, pleased that they were now fighting *for* their relationship in a way that had also brought the therapist back on board. The therapy proceeded at a new, more satisfactory pace. The new ability of both sides to pull hard on the other for a needed response or surge of energy was utilized often.

Collegial Support

Our belief in partnership extends beyond therapy to other relationships. As therapists, we believe strongly in the need for therapists to support, challenge, and encourage one another. Developing a network (formal or informal) of professionals who work to bring out the best in themselves and each other seems natural and necessary to us. As therapists, we need to expand our experience of openness, creativity, and partnership. The therapist with no access to a trusted forum (individual or group) for releasing some of the pressures and issues that therapy raises is in the same position as an isolated client. Partnership cannot be entirely one-sided. We need to remind ourselves of the terrors and joys of "turning oneself in" to someone you trust and letting them help you solve a problem.

The following example of this comes from our colleague, Sharon Beckman-Brindley. As a long-standing member of our group, she has been on both sides of the partnership dance many times. She shares a helpful example of the process of using colleagues in several ways.

"Fog Busting"   The identified patient was a dramatic, histrionic 18-year-old girl, who was referred because she slept all day,

refused to go to school, cut on herself with scissors, and talked of suicide. She had virtually no friends, although she achieved fairly well at school and was in a rock group.

Her parents had been divorced for about a year; the bitterness of their marriage persisted between them and overflowed to the children. Both Maria and her younger sister, Alice, were caught in the constant crossfire between their parents. They alternated between outright hatred and vilification of their father, and efforts to placate and become close to him. Their mother, with whom they lived, was a recovering alcoholic, who was attentive to their needs in the present but who had not been available to them emotionally when they were younger. She had been distracted by her stormy marriage, her drinking, and her limited recovery from her own severely inadequate and abusive family of origin.

My first interventions focused on giving the mother a voice with her ex-husband and on helping the parents move their children out of their still-violent battleground. Maria was hospitalized because of her self-mutilation and suicidal thoughts. Initial work with boundaries was very successful as both parents stopped their fighting over the children and began to build their own, much more appropriate individual relationships with Maria and her sister. Where they (and I) stumbled was in the next step. I consulted our group twice on this case.

The first time I brought the case to the group, I was trying to build more connectedness within the better defined mother-daughters family. Over the weeks, our sessions fizzled. One person wouldn't come because she was sick, or asleep, or forgot. If they all were present, as soon as one would speak, the others would drift away until we all were in our own fogs. They could bring energy to criticizing the father as villain, but none to one another, except in outrageous acting out and fighting. I was either exhausting myself as referee or falling asleep. When I presented the case to the group, no one there could get a feel for how to proceed either. Steve Greenstein suggested the unusual idea of asking someone to come into a therapy session and help me. I backed away, because it violated my expectations. I was supposed to be told what to do and then do it. The concept of help or support was foreign, and I felt like a failure if I needed it. At the same time, I could see that something vital was missing from the sessions. I decided to ask Dave to come in.

A few minutes into the session, Dave said to me, "Sharon, Maria is trying to speak to her mother, and it's not working. Why aren't you helping her?" This was it: He had seen precisely the moment where the sessions began to drift off, and I hadn't even noticed it until he mentioned it. I laughed and said, "I don't think I can!" Clearly, there were some issues here for me about going towards a marginally available mother. Rather than going into those, Dave merely reassured me that of course I could, and gave me nonverbal support to move in. I moved closer to Maria. I talked with her about what she was trying to say and helped her clarify and strengthen it. Then, with Dave's guidance, I moved to the arm of the couch right behind her and supported her while she talked to mom. The fogginess was gone, the directness and contact were back. It was a sweet moment and a breakthrough for all of us.

A month later, I sought from the group a second consultation. The mother had been struggling to find a strong enough voice that would command Maria's attention and interrupt her histrionic dramas. All I could do (again) was to *tell* her what to do; I found it impossible to get behind mom (in this case) and insist that she do better. Like her, I was terrified of violence and high energy. Both of us would become overly intellectual, emotionally shut down, and paralyzed as Maria would begin to spiral off.

Steve turned up the heat as he watched the tape and heard the story. "Back mother up until she gets Maria to stop," he told me. "Just *do* it!" This broke through my intellectual view of things, but I could feel myself freeze in front of the group. Others felt it, too, and asked me about it. We processed my reaction some, and then they suggested that I share my own story and terror with mom. I should tell her some about my history and how much violence terrified me and how I understood how hard it was. I did. The mother and I spent a session just talking to each other about our retreat from confrontation. Once again, it was powerful and touching. I made it clear to mom that I understood how hard it was *and* that I was totally with her. (And, if I needed help, our group was with me!) I also said that she needed to change. I said that my job was to support her *good* mothering and that I would be with her all the way. I now had a real conviction that she could be there for her children in ways that weren't available to any of us not so long ago. There was a powerful connection between us that helped to energize mom both to do what she needed to do and to allow me to provide help and support when she needed it.

We went on for six more months. There were many more dramas, and ups and downs, but always these occurred in the context of real relatedness and caring. I occasionally still see Maria's mother on the street. Maria is doing wonderfully in college. There is still a warmth between her mother and me and a shared caring that pleases us both and that continues to bring energy into both of our lives.

We have often referred to our group of colleagues as a "cuddle group" because of the great deal of support it offers each of us. But, as with a good partnership in the therapy room, you want more than just cheerleading when you feel stuck; the support must include challenge and guidance so that you can become unstuck. What the consultation offered Sharon was both clarity about her misstep and a reminder of her underlying competence as a way to help her back to a productive path. Both of those are needed; neither one by itself fully empowers people to make the changes they want to make.

It is the attention to partnership that makes the whole competence endeavor possible. Without the spirit of partnership, the challenge to grow becomes a criticism; the map of a proactive step becomes a directive; the call for courage becomes a dare. Partnership begins with the reworking of psychopathology. As we work with clients to see their problems as part of a larger process with both functional and dysfunctional aspects, we alter our relationship to them in a fundamental way. That change continues throughout therapy, and is key in making it possible to take the subsequent steps that we have outlined. The sense of connection, in which the therapist collaborates fully without surrendering his role of providing guidance and wisdom, is crucial to every aspect of a competence approach. The relationship between therapist and client has always been the heart of therapy. It still is, for us. But a competence approach, with its emphasis on challenge, mastery, and belonging, depends on a powerful, largely nonhierarchical partnership that offers maximum support for the process of striving.

LESSONS FROM CHILDREN

If a child tells a lie, tell him that he has told a lie, but don't call him a liar.

— *Jean Paul Richter*

THE CONCEPT OF COMPETENCE was largely born out of watching children master their world. Any good observer must be impressed, as White was, with the enormous energy children spend on managing the environment effectively. They engage in many tasks with no reward except for the intrinsic one of success in the encounter. They look for new challenges and respond to new stimuli out of their inherent interest in mastery. Children are extremely interested in all kinds of possibilities and in what they can do with those possibilities. The competence focus is based on that intrinsic interest in mastery, which lasts all one's life.

The question of how to bring that desire for mastery directly into therapy with children is something of a special case. The process of engaging children directly in an undertaking that will alter their plight requires some specific attention. While it is quite like the process with families, it tends to be more direct and more dependent on picking up the child's language. The "project" that we described in Chapter 3 is central. A focal undertaking is very effective with children. They have a real interest in it. For a project to give them a map and act as a lightning rod for their energy, however, it must engage them via their own words and concepts. Finding the version of the proactive step that will catch their interest and affect their behavior deserves some special examples.

"Letting the Tiger Out of the Bag"   Lisa was eight years old when she was brought in for negativism, sullenness, and school problems. Her unhappiness was especially focused around her father's new wife. She lived with them, as her mother's choice had been to start over alone out west after the divorce, and Frank was glad to keep their only child. He had married Susan about 18 months after the breakup. Lisa, five-and-a-half when her mother left, and seven when Frank and Susan married, had never grown close to Susan. Susan was certainly more interested in Frank than in Lisa, but she seemed open to and interested in getting a better relationship going with her new stepdaughter.

The therapist needed time first to help Lisa relax and feel safe. She was nonverbally and even overtly hostile when the family met together, and he did not want to rush the relationship process. Lisa and he met alone next, and planned six sessions together. They decided on six by talking about what it would take for her to "get to know him," and he was happy to let her take charge of that process. In addition to talking and playing together over that time, he discussed with her what helped her feel at ease with him and what did not. (The obvious corollary to life with Susan went unmentioned.) A number of themes came up: She liked to be perfect, she was afraid to be mad, she didn't trust that he would naturally like her, and—strongest of all—it was very hard for her to talk about her mother because she assumed that people would not understand why her mother left. The projection in this was obvious: She did not understand why her mother had left. But so was the pride and connection that Lisa felt towards her absent mother. She might not really understand her mother's absence, but she was not about to criticize her, or let Susan do so.

After several sessions in which the therapist was able to get comfortable with the central issues, he said to her, "I think you don't want to get friendly with Susan because you think she'll be critical of your mother. I think you don't want to hear *one bad word* about your mother from her! So you're not going to talk to her about *anything*!" She responded with a "Yes, and . . . " kind of response that is the best reception an interpretation ever gets. She talked about Susan "thinking she's so great" and "coming in here and taking over my family, like it's so easy." "And maybe you want to show her," the therapist said, "That it's *not* so easy. And that she can't do as good as your mom did!" "That's right," Lisa answered, "And she'll see that my mom was a good mom. She'll wonder how my mom did so well and never had any trouble with me."

So now the cat was out of the bag—actually, *a* cat, since you never know for sure if there might be other issues of equal or greater importance still afoot. Her bad behavior was a shared secret with a clear purpose. The therapist wanted to help Lisa find an active response that could alter the impasse. The insight begged to be used. So he said to her, "I'm glad you're sticking up for your mom like such a tiger. Your loyalty is great. But I worry that it's not going to work: Susan might think that if you're hard to raise, it's your mother's fault. She might think your mother raised a brat, when really she raised a tiger." Lisa was very struck with this worry. She tried to suggest that her being hard to raise would just reflect on Susan, but clearly she didn't believe it. So they started to plan how she could teach Susan that she was a tiger, not a brat.

The basic goal was to help Lisa make good use of her anger and her strength. She and the therapist decided that the same strength and determination that led her mother to homestead alone out west led Lisa to defend her mother's honor back east, at any price to herself. She decided that, with the therapist's help, she would tell Susan that she never wanted to hear anything bad about her mother (which Susan had in fact done before). She also decided to tell Susan that she was a tiger and that tigers don't let new animals into the pack easily (a fact the therapist supplied, with no idea if it was true or not) and that she, Lisa, would have to go slow in letting Susan in—*very* slow. Lisa was promised complete support in getting these things across, and the parents were brought back in after only four of the six sessions, at Lisa's request. Lisa used the therapist well and moved toward Susan directly and appropriately, with good results.

One thing that must be stated about this case is that this competence maneuver—helping Lisa develop a proactive move to change the impasse—is a beginning, not a full solution. By translating her anger and withdrawal into an active challenge she could be proud of, instead of into withdrawal and resentment, the therapist made use of her distress. That began a healthier process, but it left several issues untouched. What about her own anger towards her mother? How will she get close to Susan? Where does dad fit in the triangle? How to resolve her grief about her mother's leaving? Those questions were not addressed initially in the proactive undertaking.

Once a healthy proactive process is started, however, it tends to cause a landslide of other issues. Lisa began with the "tiger" theme, but her success seemed to strengthen her. She went on to deal in some way with many of the issues the therapist had worried about missing. Once she had learned how to challenge Susan directly and work with her without feeling disloyal to her mother, the other issues were relatively easy to engage. Lisa had developed a voice that could be used with Susan (and anyone else), and it began to serve her well in the family.

What's Pathological?

Children learn by engaging in a lot of different ideas and behaviors, including quite a few bad ones. Any of us, with bad luck, could have been caught in various acts which could be seen as psychopathological if taken at face value. It is the norm among children to engage in a large array of "disturbed" behaviors. They steal, they lie, they engage in inappropriate sexual practices, they manipulate others, they have bizarre and unrealistic fears and fantasies. We know that all of these are developmentally expectable at some points, and so common at other points so as to be of little concern. But where is the line? When is "playing doctor" a form of sexual deviance? When is "making up stories" out-and-out lying? When are "bad dreams" normal, and when are they the product of an anxiety disorder?

Certainly there are norms to serve as guidelines, and a good child therapist knows them. But there are always borderline or questionable cases. Is it natural curiosity, or is this eight-year-old boy a cross-dresser? Is this second grader highly dangerous, or was he merely experimenting with the cat's "nine lives"? The danger of a psychopathological orientation is labeling, and thus perhaps freezing, a child in a category in which he or she may not belong. It can also be dangerous, however, to ignore early signs of serious problems. If a child *is* systematically hurting animals, it is a mistake to normalize it as "experiments" and minimize the response.

The idea that any particular response is either "true psychopathology" or merely normal child's play is a false dichotomy. Almost all behaviors have both a healthy and a neurotic motive, to use Angyal's language (Chapter 4). Compulsive behavior typically develops out of a child's need to gain control of unruly impulses; hysteric behavior usually forms in response to eroticized signals in important family relationships; aggressive acting out is commonly the child's best effort to find an acceptable outlet for unacceptable levels of anger, fear, or frustration. Thus, to call any of these just pathological misses the adaptive effort, and to understand only the adaptive part can ignore the important presence of troubling or unmanageable feelings. The question is less what any single behavior *is*, than what it may *become*.

Our approach to children and their difficulties is therefore aimed quite directly at the question of the impact we can have on what their behavior becomes. We want to help children be aware of and take responsibility for their own behavior and its effects, both good and bad. This is not a simple process. Finding and developing children's competence motivation—the healthy part of their behavior, *including* the healthy part of their problematic behavior—requires creativity, flexibility and a conviction that children can change.

Children's Talents

We must always remind ourselves that children are different from adults. For our present purposes, there are a couple of specific differences that are important. First of all, children are more plastic and changeable (Combrinck-Graham, 1989). They are not as set in their ways; they are not yet convinced that they cannot change. Indeed, they are convinced that they can change, easily and often. Usually they can, and sometimes they can't, but they always believe they can.

Secondly, they don't seem to need to go back and rework things like adults do. Retrospection, introspection, insight, awareness, and working through are not as important to children as they are to adults. Patterns of behavior in children are not as ensconced or as hard to undo. More than adults, they can change just by changing, rather than needing first to gain insight and understanding. We have all seen a child make a sudden and significant change and, when asked, "What made the difference?" heard them reply, "I just wanted to." We tend to apply our theories to figure out why they changed, but sometimes those may miss the real point — they just wanted to. Children's inclination toward egocentric thinking (Elkind, 1970) and omnipotence can often work to their advantage outside the therapy context as well. For example, most children expect to have "a great year" at the beginning of school — even those with a history of failures. Capturing and realizing that kind of hope, desire, and energy are cornerstones of a competence approach. Merely taking it at face value, year after year, but not helping them to actualize it, is no help. But neither is brushing it off.

Using Children's Language

To succeed with children in therapy we must master their language, whatever it is. Adults (including therapists) often tend to try to get children to talk our language, and we lose them as a result. For example, the language of therapy is in general a language of problems and symptoms. Children do not think in terms of problems and symptoms. They look forward, not back; they think about what could be and not what was. If you ask a child why he did something wrong, he'll say, "I won't do it again." You ask about the past, but he'll tell you about the future. Children are working on becoming more than on being, and they are more interested in solutions than in problems. We adults want them to focus on problems and symptoms because that is what we have been taught to focus on. But that is not their natural focus.

Children's natural interest in competence means that they are always working on something. Therefore, if you are going to build therapy on competence and mastery, you have to give them something to master. You need to listen for their language of hopefulness and striving, and build on it. They need a focus that utilizes their sense of competence. We usually want them to work on adult issues: feelings, meaning, awareness, etc. But that is not typically a focus they understand or to which they are drawn.

"Julian the Dummy"   Julian was a six-year-old only child. Julian's father, who had been sick all of Julian's life, had recently had a very successful operation and was fully recovered. He was trying to resume leadership in the family, and Julian was strenuously resisting. From having been a major force and a quasi-adult in the family, Julian was now being pushed back to a more appropriate six-year-old position. He hated it. Julian's parents had brought him in because he was acting very badly. He was kicking and fighting in school, using swear words, and generally acting unmanageably. In the first session, a structural intervention was used to reestablish the father's control. There was a huge confrontation between Julian and the father, which the father won with the therapist's support. Julian stepped back and regrouped and started to work to reenter the family in a different position. They reported that, in the intervening week, he had done very well, but had been very quiet.

The following sequence occurred at the end of the second session. Julian had spent much of the session sitting in the therapist's lap. While the therapist's preference would have been to have him in his parents' laps, their laps were not safe for him yet. He had not yet built an emotional bridge back to them, in spite of his improved behavior. In wrapping up the session the therapist had taken a long time to focus on the parents' tasks. As he turned to wrap up with Julian, he tried to make that bridge for Julian via a push to tell his parents about all his feelings—especially his negative ones.

Therapist: (*wrapping up*) . . . and your job, Julian, is to tell mom and dad what you're feeling. They need to know whether you're sad, or mad, or upset, or scared. You have to use that "good brain" (*his phrase*) of yours to let mom and dad know what's going on, and what you're feeling, so they can help you. Right? OK? [Julian is sitting slouched down in the therapist's lap with a funny look on his face, studying himself in the one-way mirror. He refers back to an earlier moment in the session when he and the therapist had decided that he looked like a ventriloquist's dummy and played at it for a minute.]

Julian: Me want dummy again.

Th: You want to be the dummy again?

Julian: (*Nods*)

Th: OK, I'll be the ventriloquist and run your controls. (*Puts his hand on Julian's back*) Hi, Julian!

Julian: Hi!

Th: How are you today?

Julian: Great!

Th: (*To parents*) Isn't this amazing? My lips hardly move! (*To Julian*) And what are you feeling so great about?

Julian: My mom and dad!

Th: Your mom and dad!

Julian: Yup.

Th: Well, they tell me you've been very good this week. Is that true?

Julian: Yup.

Th: Well, how'd you do it?

Julian: I just did it!

Th: You just—*did it*? Just like that?

Julian: Yup. It's easy.

Th: Well, if I asked you to teach other kids how to do that, what would you tell them?

Julian: Just listen to your mom and dad, and your teachers, and do what they say.

Th: Really? That's all? Just do what they say?

Julian: Yup. And if you do what they say, then they can help you calm down and you're OK. [They talk about it some more and then Julian says goodbye while the therapist drinks water. Parents applaud.]

What Julian wanted to talk about was not feelings. He wanted to talk about the reparation work with his parents: about being a good boy and what he'd learned about calming down and not throwing fits and having temper tantrums. The ventriloquism ruse, which he brings to the therapist, was a wonderful way for them to work together. Julian could pretend that this was just a dummy speaking. The therapist could sit there and rub his back and "work his controls." Julian needed a camouflage for his reentry. When the therapist tried to get Julian to speak his language, nothing was accomplished. Finally, Julian taught the therapist to speak his. There is an old Zen saying, "When the pupil is ready, the teacher will appear"; Julian appeared even before the pupil was ready.

Possibilities

Children's improvement, in general, does not hinge on insight and working through. It hinges on the plasticity of their behavior and trying different things until something works. Children are full of possibilities; they believe anything is possible. Tomorrow will be better, their homework will get done, they'll hit a home run the next time up. That plasticity keeps them going and hoping and trying new things. Those are crucial strengths for children, because they have to absorb a lot of failure and disappointment.

Having some hope that things are going to get better and move forward is a vital part of their survival and one that deserves our support. Yet trusting that plasticity of children's behavior is a bit of a gamble. Where with adults we are apt to go back over the recursive pattern of dysfunction, their vision, and the proactive step, with children we often have to jump in and take our chances. Because they're not interested in problems, we often have to move towards a solution that harnesses the underlying healthy urge. We look for ways to translate that impulse into a healthy form rather than quash the impulse.

"From Fighter to Lover"   Tyrone, a 10-year-old fourth grader, was in constant trouble in school for fighting. In fact, when he

graduated from preschool, he was known as "the biter," and from kindergarten on he was known as a fighter. He was so bad that the school was now considering placing him in an emotionally disturbed class. He had his own special chair in the principal's office, which he visited almost daily. His mother objected to his being placed in an ED class and agreed instead to come to family therapy. Also in the family were two younger sisters, who were not involved in the therapy. The family had few resources, lived in public housing, and the mother worked two jobs to try to "make something of herself." The family missed two appointments before coming in 30 minutes late for the third one. Mother announced that they could only come occasionally, due to work demands.

The therapist, in spite of her irritation, realized she had to work hard to make a good connection. She looked for where Tyrone wanted to be different. He told her that he really wanted to do better, but saw no alternative to fighting; that was just the way he had to do it. He said, "I've never started a fight in my life. The teacher always looks when I throw a punch. She never sees that the other guy throws the first punch." (We're still waiting for the child that comes in and says, "I'm your man. I'm the one who throws that first punch. I go from class to class. Lock me up.") Tyrone said he was always the one who got caught, talked to by the teacher, and then yanked up to the principal's office to be talked to some more.

Though this injustice sounds improbable, in order to identify the healthy striving in children, a therapist really needs to understand what the problem feels like *to them*. It is only through respecting their hurt, pain, anger, or sense of injustice that you are going to be able to acknowledge that they are not getting what they want. Then you can begin to challenge their pattern without challenging the person. Tyrone readily agreed that he had an undeserved bad reputation. But, he also poignantly talked about being resigned to it.

With some probing from the therapist, however, he was also able to talk about some other parts of himself. For example, in addition to being a successful fighter, he also saw himself as a "cool guy" and a lady's man. He said, in quite a flirtatious way to the therapist, that he had several girlfriends and that girls always liked him. In fact, he shared with her his cardinal rule, which he had never broken: No matter how aggravating your girlfriend is, you don't hit her. He said, "Loving and fighting don't mix." Here was the therapist's entry point.

Tyrone's fighting was connected to both his underlying anger with the world *and* to a healthy impulse to be top dog at something. He wanted to make a name for himself, to be seen as cool. He was doing it the only way he knew how to do it. So the therapist came up with a different theme for him. Since he was now 10 and in the fourth grade, she suggested that maybe he was getting too old and too cool to fight. Since loving and fighting don't mix, she suggested, he might want to be known as a lover, not a fighter.

The therapist first introduced this idea to Tyrone alone, and talked to him about it, and he signed on enthusiastically. But he had no idea how this could be done. They decided that he would get his mother's help with this change. What follows is the therapist presenting this idea to Tyrone and his mother and having Tyrone ask his mom to help him change his reputation. Children love themes and undertakings. If we suggested he change his reputation by not fighting, that would not have held much interest for him. All his life, every significant adult had told him to stop fighting, with no visible effect. But he thought the idea of becoming a lover *instead of* a fighter was intriguing. That theme got him interested in changing.

Therapist: Tyrone and I've been talking and we thought maybe what we'd work on was changing his reputation—from a "fighter" to a "lover."

Mother: Uh huh! Well now!

Th: He gets into a lot of trouble because of his bad reputation. Something happens in class and, if he's around, he gets blamed. But I've seen another side of Tyrone—his respect for girls, for instance. He's got a girlfriend. She passes him notes and calls him.

Mother: Oh yeah.

Tyrone: In the cafeteria, too, she's looking at me—she and her friends. She's crazy, man. She likes me a lot.

Th: Yeah, I'm like her. I see a lot of positives in Tyrone, and they're getting overshadowed by his bad reputation. People are missing what a "lover" he can be. So, he thought he might like to learn to show that side of himself more . . . but he's not sure how. He was wondering if you could help.

Tyrone: Yeah. Can you help me, Mom?

Mother: Sure—it's something you can do, Tyrone. I know you're a nice boy. I can see good in you. I like this idea because it's you doing it—not me telling you.

Th: And when people see that Tyrone's a lover and not a fighter, they'll know he's not fighting because he's too cool to fight. He's above that.

Tyrone: Yeah, too cool to fight.

Th: So, what are some specific, concrete ways he can change his reputation? Can we work on that? Let's start at school, because that's what's giving him the most trouble.

Mother: Tyrone can come up with them.

Tyrone: I don't have any ideas . . . I don't know nothing much . . . not unless . . . listen to the teacher.

Mother: That's one, right there.

Tyrone: Write whatever the teacher's got on the chalkboard.

Mother: That's two.

Tyrone: And do whatever the teacher tells me to do.

Mother: That's three.

It is always amazing how well children know the classroom rules, even when they don't follow them!

This was fine as far as it went, but children need more than talk. Their natural language is play and action. They can often progress more by doing than they can by talking. Here, Tyrone is just talking. So the therapist asked the mother if she would practice testing Tyrone's new resolve to be "too cool to fight." She said she was too shy; she'd be glad to try it at home, but not here. So the therapist practiced with him how to do it. She instructed Tyrone that she was going to be picking on him and that he was to take that picking just as long as he could; then, he was to decide whether he should fight back or call the teacher, Mrs. Grant, for help. Calling the teacher for help was something Tyrone had never done in his life, but it was a useful component of his new identity. Lovers, he was told, can use anyone they want to get uncool fighters out of their way. They have more important business to attend to than fighting jerks.

Th: (*grabs Tyrone's coat off his lap*)

Tyrone: Give me my coat!

Th: (*poking his leg*) I'm not giving you anything. You're too chicken to hit me back. Chicken Flicken!

Tyrone: Give me back my coat! Stop stepping on my coat!

Mother: (*whispering to Tyrone*) That's it. You're doing good.

Th: Make me! (*keeps poking Tyrone and throws his coat on the ground*)

Tyrone: Yes—I'm gonna tell the teacher on you.

Th: No one's gonna believe you. *You're* gonna get in trouble. You're the bad one around here. (*keeps poking and hitting Tyrone's leg*) Chicken! (*makes chicken noises*) Chicken! You're too scared to fight now, chicken!

Tyrone: Give me my coat! (*looks over at mother, she nods approval*)

Th: Nope! I'm gonna throw it in the street and let the truck run over it.

Tyrone: Quit throwing my coat, quit hitting me—*MS. GRANT!!* I'm telling the teacher, and I'm *not* fighting. Ms. Grant!

Tyrone told his mother later that he was sure this therapist was absolutely crazy, but that she had some good ideas.

There was plenty of work to be done following this. As with Lisa, this is a beginning, not a whole solution. The therapist contacted Tyrone's teacher and spent some time with her to make sure that she was going to be attentive to, and appreciative of, Tyrone's new reputation. She, by the way, was delighted with the idea that her little hellion was going to become a lover in the classroom and not a fighter. This new theme regalvanized her energy for Tyrone, and she became his ardent supporter. This became a real turning point for Tyrone. Finally, somebody had seen the other side of his fighting and had helped him find a way to move away from fighting, *and toward something* that worked to meet the same needs. The energy that he had been using to prove what a successful fighter he was could now be directed into what a good lover he could be.

"Kadeem Runs the Numbers"   Often, to build children's competence we have to follow their energy and slowly turn it to our purposes. We have to meet them halfway and forge a project that links their needs with ours.

Kadeem was a very unhappy five-year-old. His parents had divorced two years previously. He missed his dad tremendously, and his mother was very busy, having just started graduate school. In his preschool, he had been starting fights, hitting other kids, and most recently "mooned" the entire class at nap time. He was angry and needy, but he could not talk to his mother or the therapist. Nor would he talk about how he was behaving, or the time-outs that were becoming the main event in his life. It had become increasingly hard for him to deal directly with any of those things. Like five-year-olds everywhere, he could always blunt a probe if he did not like where it is going; any distraction would do it. He would make farting noises with his mouth or throw things around the room or whatever he had to do to get the therapist off the track—"the track" being the problems and the feelings the therapist wanted to talk about. Yet, it was clear that he was in distress and was taking the distress out in an inappropriate way, which was making trouble for him and for the classroom.

While the therapist wanted to help him deal with his distress, Kadeem was not interested in that. What he *was* interested in was numbers. He loved writing numbers. He had made the numbers 1 through 20 in a variety of marker colors on the therapist's big pad during much of the session. So the therapist started to follow his energy and lead, by playing numbers with him while also looking for a connecting point. It became clear that what he liked was the orderliness and the progression of numbers. The therapist decided to try to play with him about that and see if he could weave Kadeem's distress, the moods and the feelings, and Kadeem's energy, the orderliness of the numbers, together.

The therapist started to tie the numbers into a sort of loose scale of good days and bad days. He used the numbers as ratings of what those days would be like. A zero would be the best day (to conform to zero time-outs), and the worst day would be a five. As they played with that idea, Kadeem clearly liked the scaling part of it. He used colors and size of numerals to carry meaning. For example he drew a large 5 in red because he said, "Red is a mad color and when I'm in a 5 day, I'm really feeling mad." And he made zero blue because, "Blue's in the American flag, and I'm proud of America." It became increasingly meaningful to him because it was connected to what he had interest and energy for. He was pleased also that the therapist would work with the scaling that he loved.

Toward the end of the session, after working on it off and on for 30 minutes, the therapist wanted to finish up the scale and put some action into it.

Therapist: So now we have all those beautiful numbers, all in a row on the pad here, and we need to remember what they mean. So this is . . .

Kadeem: Zero! And zero is a no time-out day, when I'm feeling good and my teacher is nice! And this is 1, and I would just get one time-out. If I do something not good, that the teacher doesn't like. And 2, if I do two things. But 2 is not *too* bad.

Th: No, 2 is not too bad. That might be a day when you make some mistakes. What about this one?

Kadeem: 3 is more time-outs, it's not good. When I have three time-outs I am orange, because it's not a good day like if I am mad at mommy or my teacher. Or if mommy left my drink out of my lunch. Or she's late.

Th: You hate that when she's late, or forgets stuff, eh? That makes you mad, and mad gets you time-outs?

Kadeem: Yes. Three or maybe four or five or *100*! (*Loud*)

Th: Sometimes you *really* get mad!

Kadeem: Yes, I get so mad I do stuff the teacher doesn't like *at all*, and I . . . I make . . . it's not . . .

Th: You can't even *say* it, it makes you so mad! I'll bet you get *very* mad!

Kadeem: Yes! I do! Sometimes I get five time-outs because everything is terrible, and I miss my dad and a dinosaur bites me!

Th: A dinosaur . . . ?

Kadeem: Yes and everything is terrible!

Th: Yes and you're mad at everyone some days! And those days get a huge, red 5, because you feel red-mad on those days!

Kadeem: And I get five time-outs!

Th: And that might be when you're missing your dad . . .

Kadeem: I miss him every day, but sometimes I miss him the most. And sometimes my teacher doesn't let me eat my lunch . . .

There were several interesting things in this sequence. One was that Kadeem and the therapist started talking about all of the feelings *and tying them to the numbers*, and Kadeem really liked that. He hated talking about his feelings *per se*, but he liked it in this format. He really went into the differences, from 5 to 0. Another important thing is that one of the problems that we therapists often introduce into therapy with children is that we want to talk only about the problems and the bad feelings. We are much more interested in the 4 and 5 days than the 0 days. Children want to talk about the 0 and 1 days because they are so proud of when they feel good and do well. We have to be willing to talk to them about the whole range — as much about the days that they are wonderful and perfect as the others. A third important aspect of this session was its playful, down-to-earth nature. Therapist and child emoted and talked about the feelings and made them real, touchable things that could be dealt with, in a playful way. They were talking about real events, which was much more appealing than talking about abstract feelings.

The outcome of the session was that Kadeem and the therapist made a gloriously large chart that listed the days on the ordinate, and 0 to 5 on the abscissa. Before school each day, Kadeem was to predict which kind of day he would have. This big chart was to go up on the refrigerator. This was not an attempt at charting and behavior modification, but rather a way of helping him think, "How am I feeling?" "What's going on with me?" The idea was not that he have all 0 days, but that he try to predict how he would be; that he have a way to reflect on his feelings that he liked.

What happens if he predicts wrong? It doesn't matter. It is not the product that is of interest, just the process of thinking about it and talking about it. If he predicts a 0 and gets three time-outs, then he and mom have some very interesting things to talk about in a way he can understand. We want to say, "You miss your dad, you're sad about the divorce, you don't understand why he had to leave." In time, we may be able to do that. In talking about the numbers and making his predictions, he may get into why he feels bad, but he may very well not. In either case, he has a new language (mostly his own) for working on his behavior — one that he could enjoy and get excited about. He worked very well with it and took pride and interest in his chart and his accuracy.

Which Way to Move?

One of the dilemmas we face with a proactive, movement-oriented approach is deciding which way to move. Can we help this child become more competent by moving with her into her struggle with the pain, the anger, or the sadness, or by moving her away from the struggle towards more developmentally appropriate behavior? The answer is — it depends. It depends on whether the child's voice needs strengthening or redirecting. If, like Tyrone, she is not saying what she wants (what he really wanted was to be a success, not a fighter), then you move her away from the problem behavior to something that she can master. You tap the part of the child that has more potential for success. If, on the other hand, significant others are not paying attention to the child's message, and this message needs to be heard and can lead to mastery, then you move with her into the pain and hurt so she will feel able to say it more clearly.

The first step with either move is making sure you acknowledge and understand the child's view of her dilemma. It is only then that you will know whether to support that energy or redirect it.

"April Storms"   April was a very bright, articulate seven-year-old girl who, with her family, came in for a second round of family therapy. The family consisted of the two parents, an older brother, and a younger sister called May. Nine months earlier, this family had come when April was out of control. She had come in and taken over the office, bossing everyone around. At that time, the therapist got the parents back in charge of the family

and helped them to control her tantrums, set some rules, and be consistent. While April was initially outraged, she settled down after several weeks of really good testing and started to do well. The parents became comfortable with being in charge, and therapy ended after eight sessions.

They returned nine months later because the parents were worried that the "anger problem" was resurfacing. April had been away at summer camp for a month and, since returning, had been increasingly difficult to manage. She always seemed angry and had started having tantrums again, though not as bad as before. One of the old patterns that was known from the previous work was that April adored her father and felt ambivalent toward her mother. She not only adored him, she really wanted mother out of the picture so that she and dad could sail off into the sunset. Twice, she had asked her father very seriously if he would consider running away with her. And she knew that if things got tense enough around the house, her mother would feel unappreciated and pull back, while her father would move in and take over with her. The therapist knew she did not have any corresponding way to get close to her mother.

Underlying this oedipal struggle was the healthy urge to be connected in a special way to someone. She wanted a partner, somebody to whom she could be special and vice versa. The urge was fine, it was just wrongly fixated on only one parent. What the therapist did in this sequence was to try to help her find another direction: Could she find specialness with mother?

In this, the first session of the second therapy, April had labeled her new problem. She said, "I'm not completely out of control now like I was. But I'm grumpy. I get a real mean look on my face. I can't help myself and then I find myself saying mean and awful things and getting in trouble. I don't like it." Note that this is developmental progress; she had moved away from the tactics of a two-year-old (temper tantrums) to grouchy and hostile interactions that fit an older child better. She was encouraged to ask her family for their ideas about her grumpy problem. Her brother suggested that she simply stop being grumpy, but April was a mover and a shaker, and the idea of walking away from something held no interest for her. Like Tyrone, she needed something to move towards, not just away from. So the therapist began looking for something that would hold more interest for her.

April turned next to her father but the therapist blocked this and directed her toward her mother for advice. Could her mother, who was already an expert at dealing with grumpiness (April's and her father's), become April's advisor? Could April learn to go to her for a consultation when she felt a grump attack coming on, rather than having to face it alone? In that way she could move closer to her mother, using her as a partner, instead of seeing her as the competition.

Therapist: Who in the family is best at not being grumpy? Who is best at being nice?

April: My dad and mom.

Th: Tell me about your mom. How do people see her?

April: I don't know. Nice, I guess.

Th: Well, it strikes me that she's really good at being nice. In fact, she's like an expert at being soft and sweet. People really like her. She says nice things a lot, and it looks like it's pretty easy for her.

April: Yeah. It is. She's always nice except when she's mad at me.

Th: I wonder if learning to be nice is something you would like to learn to be better at, being soft and sweet rather than grumpy. Because if you're soft and sweet, you wouldn't have time to be grumpy.

April: Yeah, but how do I learn to be soft and sweet?

Th: Let's get your mom to teach you. Invite her over to sit with you on the couch. And let's ask the guys to leave because these will be *private* soft and sweet lessons. (*April giggles and orders the guys out; mom immediately hugs April and lets her nestle in.*)

April: (*to mom*) How can I learn to be soft and sweet?

Mom: Well, how about if I teach you? How about when I notice that you're starting to get grumpy, I bring you under my wing like this (*cuddles her*) and say, "You're there again. What can you do instead?"

April: I always like getting under your wing. That's comfortable.

Th: So, mom could be your soft and sweet coach.

April: Yeah (*to mom*), and when I'm feeling grumpy, I could come ask you to teach me how to be soft and sweet. I could come get under your wing.

Mom: Yes, and I'll whisper some ideas to you. I'm going to teach you all these things I know.

The pull toward belonging is a strong urge for all of us, but it is especially urgent for children. When children have problems, they often become disconnected from their parents. Parents become policemen. They monitor, they catch, they punish. Creating a more healing connection between parents and their children helps them *both* reorganize their energy. The child is responsible for behaving differently, but is no longer alone in the struggle. The parent is helped to take charge, but in a way that emphasizes connection more than control. Healing comes in large part from learning to be in relationships differently.

A follow-up with this family revealed that April did very well at using her mother, especially when grumpy. In one incident they described, the father got mad at April, and she rolled her eyes, walked over to her mother, put an arm around her, and said, "I tell you, I don't know how to handle that man! I need a lesson!"

Direct Moves

The kind of direct move that was made with April, and that we make with children fairly often, is very important. In therapy training, and perhaps play therapy training in particular, direct moves are against the rules. One is not supposed to encourage specific changes. Children theoretically cannot just go from point A to point B. But, with April, the therapist created direct access to the mother. She said to April very directly, "Your mom is an expert on not letting grumpiness run your life, and it's something you need to learn from her. She is going to help you learn." April picked it up nicely and said, "I love getting under your wing." It was a lovely expression, like her mother was a brood hen, a force to be made use of. April learned from an absolutely direct push how to move closer to her mother.

Expanding people's repertoires is important. Helping people to understand the ruts they are in, and to have the courage to move out of their ruts, is always important. However, we expand people's repertoires best not just by helping them see old patterns and new possibilities, but by helping them actually make the moves. We try hard in training to undermine the fear of direct moves, since direct interactions are the heart of mastery. The greatest human failure, our self-imposed prison, lies in not reaching out, not trying to improve our relationship matrix. Reaching out involves some risk, but when we create momentum, there is a healthy process that kicks in. The healthy part of the person is activated. We try to get the momentum going and expand the repertoire, and to get the child interested in his own potential for differentness.

The fundamental issue here is building momentum towards, and keeping a clear focus on, what the child can do to change his plight. What can he engage in of a healthy, developmentally appropriate nature that will help him move to a better spot? This approach makes it easy to get children interested, because the idea of being in a better spot, even briefly, is inherently interesting to kids. They will almost always try a project if it is relevant, understandable, and doable. They *want* to try new things. They want to move in new directions and accept new challenges. So, if we can make doing better fit that description, they are doubly interested in trying it. The therapist needs to use his heart and his playfulness to find a place from which the child can move forward. He needs to believe in the power of mastery, and then *give them something they can master*.

Our interest in competence and courage began with observing children's fierce desire for mastery. As we learned to help children make progress towards competence in their families, our interest in the mechanisms by which this happens grew. Children, with their open-hearted and hopeful nature, make an ideal laboratory for learning about vital processes in all of us. As we observed and honed our work with children, the mechanisms that enhance their journey towards competence became clearer. For example, it is easiest to see in children both their health and their pathology. The striving for mastery and belonging that lurks behind most symptoms is most apparent in children. We also learned from children about the importance of hope and vision in clinical work.

Not only are children often the ones who keep hope alive in families; they have also taught us, by their comfort with projects and proactive steps, how much people can move in a healthy direction, given a positive focus and strong support. Children are natural risk-takers, sometimes out of faith in the world and sometimes out of desperation. Their energy and their eagerness to make the world work have provided us with both motivation and lessons for bringing courage into therapy.

Finally, children taught us the value of partnership in any endeavor. We accept as a given children's need for partnership, and we find ways to offer it when they have lost either their connection with helpers or, worse, their hope for such a connection. The natural partnership we felt with children became a model for such partnership with all clients. This is different from our own training in rapport; it is different from advice-giving; it is different from parenting. All those are appropriate at times with children, but they are not the model for therapy. The partnership we learned in pursuing competence with children taught us a new model of close collaboration and theme-building. When that works, there is a synergistic process in which the child's natural energy and courage are brought to life by the therapist and set on the path toward competence.

Having learned this from children, it was a small step to bring this same process to bear on clinical encounters of all kinds. Adults, too, are developing and growing and need productive endeavors—especially within their families. While it is sometimes harder to tap their genuine hopefulness than it is with children, it is there. It deserves recognition and encouragement.

Part of the appeal for us of the concepts of competence and courage is that they are fundamental and universal. We never worry that they do not exist at all in a person, only that they are so deeply buried that we cannot reach them. As therapists, we continue to struggle with new ways to reach the healthy striving in everyone.

REFERENCES

American Psychiatric Association (1987). *Diagnostic and statistical manual of mental disorders* (3rd ed., rev). Washington, DC: Author.

Bandura, A. (1990). Conclusion: Reflections on nonability determinants of competence. In R. Sternberg & J. Kolligian (Eds.), *Competence considered* (pp. 315–362). New Haven: Yale University Press.

Berenson, D. (1992). Personal communication.

Boszormenyi-Nagy, I. (1987). *Foundations of contextual therapy.* New York: Brunner/Mazel.

Campbell, J. (1990). *The hero with a thousand faces.* New York: World Publishing.

Campbell, J. (1988). *The power of myth.* New York: Doubleday.

Combrinck-Graham, L. (1989). Family models of childhood psychopathology. In L. Combrinck-Graham (Ed.), *Children in family contexts: Perspectives on treatment* (pp. 67–89). New York: Guilford.

Cowen, E. (1991). In pursuit of wellness. *American Psychologist, 46,* 404–408.

de Shazer, S. (1985). *Keys to solution in brief therapy.* New York: W. W. Norton.

de Shazer, S. (1991). *Putting difference to work.* New York: W. W. Norton.

Dweck, C. S. (1986). Motivational processes affecting learning. *American Psychologist, 41,* 1040–1048.

Elkind, D. (1970). *Children and adolescents: Interpretive essays on Jean Piaget.* New York: Oxford University Press.

Garmezy, N. (1987). Stress, competence and development: Continuities in the study of schizophrenic adults, children vulnerable to psychopathology, and the search for stress-resistant children. *American Journal of Orthopsychiatry, 57,* 159–174.

Greenstein, Steve (1992). Personal communication.

Haley, J. (1973). *Uncommon therapy*. New York: W. W. Norton.

Hedin, M. (1990). The mean kid. *Family Therapy Networker, 14*: 64–68.

Hendrick, I. (1942). Instinct and the ego during infancy. *Psychoanalytic Quarterly, 11*, 33–58.

Kyi, A. S. S. (1991). Corrupted by fear. *The Washington Post*. Oct. 15, p. A23.

Leggett, E. L. (1985). Children's entity and incremental theories of intelligence: Relationships to achievement behaviors. Paper presented at the annual meeting of the Eastern Psychological Association, Boston.

Levine, S. (1990). An interview with Stephan Levine. *Inquiring mind*. Berkeley, CA: Dharma Press.

Levine, S. (1987). *Healing into life and death*. New York: Doubleday.

Licht, B. G., & Dweck, C. S. (1984). Determinants of academic achievement: The interaction of children's achievement orientations with skill area. *Developmental Psychology, 20*, 628–636.

Madanes, C. (1984). *Behind the one-way mirror*. San Francisco: Jossey-Bass.

Markus, H., Cross, S., & Wurf, E. (1990). The role of the self-system in competence. In R. J. Sternberg and J. Kolligian (Eds.), *Competence considered* (pp. 205–225). New Haven: Yale University Press.

Markus, H., & Nurius, P. (1986). Possible selves. *American Psychologist, 41*, 954–969.

Masterpasqua, F. (1991). A competence paradigm for psychological practice. *American Psychologist, 44*, 1366–1371.

Minuchin, S. (1974). *Families and family therapy*. Cambridge: Harvard University Press.

Minuchin, S., & Fishman, H. C. (1981). *Family therapy techniques*. Cambridge: Harvard University Press.

Nichols, M. (1987). *The self in the system*. New York: Brunner/Mazel.

Nichols, M., & Schwartz, R. (1991). *Family therapy: Concepts and methods* (2nd ed.). Boston: Allyn & Bacon.

O'Hanlon, W., & Weiner-Davis, M. (1989). *In search of solutions: A new direction in psychotherapy*. New York: W. W. Norton.

Papp, P. (1984). The creative leap. *Family Therapy Networker, 8*, 20–80.

Podvoll, E. (1983). Uncovering a patient's history of sanity. In J. Welwood (Ed.), *Awakening the heart: East/West approaches to psychotherapy and the healing relationship* (pp. 183–191). Boston: Shambhala.

Rogers, C. (1961). *On becoming a person*. Boston: Houghton Mifflin.

Rutter, M. (1987). Psychosocial resilience and protective mechanisms. *American Journal of Orthopsychiatry, 57*, 316–331.

Satir, V. M. (1988). *The new peoplemaking*. Palo Alto: Science and Behavior Books.

Scheinfeld, D. R. (1983). Family relationships and school achievement among boys of lower-income urban black families. *American Journal of Orthopsychiatry, 53*, 127–143.

Schwartz, R. (1988). Know thy selves. *Family Therapy Networker, 12*, 21–29.

Seligman, M. (1975). *Helplessness: On depression, development, and death*. San Francisco: Freeman.

Snyder, C. R. (1991). Hope and health. In C. R. Snyder & D. R. Forsyth (Eds.), *The handbook of social and clinical psychology* (pp. 285–305). New York: Pergamon Press.

Sroufe, L. A. (1983). Infant-caregiver attachment and patterns of adaptation in preschool: The roots of maladaptation and competence. In M. Perlmutter (Ed.), *Minnesota symposium on child psychiatry* (Vol. 16). Minneapolis: University of Minnesota Press.

Sroufe, L. A. (1978). Attachment and the roots of competence. *Human Nature*, October, pp. 50–57.

Sternberg, R., & Kolligian, J. (Eds.)(1990). *Competence considered.* New Haven: Yale University Press.

Strayhorn, J. (1988). *The competent child: An approach to psychotherapy and preventive mental health.* New York: Guilford.

Thompson, J. R. (1987). *The process of psychotherapy: An integration of clinical experience and empirical research.* Lanham, MD: University Press of America.

Waters, E., & Sroufe, L. A. (1983). Social competence as a developmental construct. *Developmental review, 3,* 79–97.

Watzlawick, P., Weakland, J., & Fisch, R. (1974). *Change: Principles of problem formation and problem resolution.* New York: W. W. Norton.

Webster (1968). *Webster's new twentieth century dictionary, unabridged.* New York: World Publishing Company.

White, M., & Epston, D. (1990). *Narrative means to therapeutic ends.* New York: W. W. Norton.

White, R. (1959). Motivation reconsidered: The concept of competence. *Psychological Review, 66,* 297–333.

Wylie, M. (1990). Brief therapy on the couch. *Family Therapy Networker, 14,* 26–35.

Index